The Minor Prophets

God Battling for the Heart of His People

Berean Study Series 2025

HERITAGE
CHRISTIAN UNIVERSITY
PRESS

The Minor Prophets: God Battling for the Hearts of His People

Published by Heritage Christian University

Copyright © 2025 by Heritage Christian University Press

Manufactured in the United States of America

Cataloging-in-Publication Data

Encountering the gospel/

Berean Study Series

p. cm.

Includes scripture index.

ISBN 978-1-956811-97-1 (pbk.) 978-1-956811-98-8 (ebook)

1. Bible. Minor Prophets—Study and teaching. 2. Christian life—Study and teaching I. Title. II. Series.

224.9007—dc20

Library of Congress Control Number: 2025931330

Cover design by Brad McKinnon and Brittany Vander Maas.

For information:

Heritage Christian University Press
3625 Helton Drive, PO Box HCU,
Florence, AL 35630
www.hcu.edu

Contents

Introduction

Bill Bagents

Their Roles

The prophets of the Old Testament were spokesmen called by God to deliver His messages. Many think that prophets primarily predicted future events. Their work involved much more, including reminding people of God's law, condemning sin, calling for repentance, warning of punishment, encouraging the faithful in times of trial, announcing God's judgment, and advising national rulers. While many prophets foretold future events, their work dealt far more with "forthtelling"—with addressing the people and situations of their own time.

Concerning forthtelling versus foretelling, Fee and Stuart assert, "Less than 2% of Old Testament prophecy is messianic. Less than 5% specifically describes the new-covenant age. Less than 1% describes events yet to come in our time."[1] Even if we can't verify their precision, their point is clear and sensible. Yet in balance and fairness, we confidently believe that Acts 18:24–28, Romans 15:4, 1 Corinthians 10:11, and 2 Timothy 3:14–17 remain both true and powerful.

In their excellent chapter "Old Testament—Prophecy," Duvall and Hays suggest that the overall message of the prophets "can be broken down to three basic points

1. You have broken covenant: you had better repent!
2. No repentance? Then judgment!
3. Yet there is hope beyond the judgment for a glorious restoration."[2]

God's Revelation

God communicated with prophets in many ways. Sometimes it was by direct speech as in Deuteronomy 34:10, Isaiah 6:8, and Jeremiah 1:9. Other methods included dreams and visions (Numbers 12:6), symbols or object lessons (Jeremiah 18), and the written word (Daniel 9:2). Whatever the means, the prophets were inspired by God to understand and reveal His word (Numbers 11:29). Any change to His revelation, whether addition or deletion, was punishable by death (Deuteronomy 18:20).

The Prophets' Methods

The prophets communicated God's message in various ways. Sermons (Jeremiah 2), parables (Isaiah 5:1–7, and allegories (Ezekiel 16) were frequently used. Ezekiel, in particular, was noted for acting out God's messages

(Ezekiel 4:1–4). Hosea literally lived his message before the people (Hosea 1:2–11). Malachi famously employed a communication form described as "the covenant lawsuit" (Malachi 1:2, 1:6, 2:13–15, 2:17, 3:8). Prophets also referred to earlier portions of the Old Testament and to proverbs that were current in their day (Daniel 9:11–13, Ezekiel 16:44). In a major sense, the prophets were both poets and preachers. They spoke and wrote with visceral poetic flare. Duvall and Hays capture this perfectly: "Amos does not simply say, 'God is mad.' Rather, he proclaims 'The lion has roared.'"[3] The prophets beg us to read them with both head and heart. They urge us to know, feel, understand, and align our lives with God's reality. Examples abound.

- "Your love is like a morning cloud, like the dew that goes early away" (Hosea 6:4).
- "Ephraim is a cake not turned" (Hosea 7:8).
- "Ephraim is like a dove: silly and without sense" (Hosea 7:11).
- "Lament like a virgin wearing sackcloth for the bridegroom of her youth" (Joel 1:8).
- Micah spoke of evil rulers, "who tear the skin from off my people, and their flesh from off their bones, who eat the flesh of my people, and flay their skin from off them, and break their bones in pieces, and chop them up like meat for the pot, like flesh in a caldron" (Micah 3:1–3).
- "I will throw filth at you and treat you with contempt and make you a spectacle. And all

who look at you will shrink from you ..." (Nahum 3:6–7).

- "I will bring distress on mankind, so they shall walk like the blind, because they have sinned against the Lord; their blood shall be poured out like dust, and their flesh like dung" (Zephaniah 1:17).
- "But they refused to pay attention and turned a stubborn shoulder and stopped their ears that they might not hear. They made their hearts diamond-hard lest they should hear the law and the words that the Lord of hosts had sent by his Spirit through the former prophets" (Zechariah 7:11–12).
- "But for you who fear my name, the sun of righteousness shall rise with healing in its wings. You shall go out leaping like calves from the stall" (Malachi 4:2).

Types of Prophets

Many prophets left no inspired writings. They are generally called the "oral prophets." These include Nathan, Elijah, and Elisha. Of the sixteen writing prophets, four are called Major Prophets, mainly because the books they wrote are longer. Calling Isaiah, Jeremiah, Ezekiel, and Daniel Major Prophets in no way implies that their writings are more inspired or more important than other inspired writings.

With the Minor Prophets, please do not misread the word "minor." It speaks primarily of the length of the books, though even that needs qualification. At approximately 9,000 words, Daniel—by far the shortest major prophet—is much closer in length to Zechariah—the longest book of the minor prophets at approximately 4,850 words—than to its fellow major prophets. Scripture does not categorize the Hebrew prophets as major and minor. That differentiation is both somewhat helpful and somewhat arbitrary. We'd be unwise to think of the Minor Prophets as minor in content, impact, or importance.

Historical Setting

The period of the writing prophets covers some 425 years between around 850 B.C. and 425 B.C. The nation of Israel split into two kingdoms upon the death of Solomon in 930 B.C. The ten northern tribes, generally called Israel or Ephraim, fell to Assyria during the time of Isaiah. The two southern tribes, generally called Judah, fell to Babylon in a series of three invasions during the ministries of Daniel, Jeremiah, and Ezekiel. The next world empire, Persia, allowed some of the Jews to return to their homeland in 536 B.C. The time of the prophets was filled with political and social upheavals.

Dating the Prophets

Exact dates of writing and the exact chronological order of the prophetic books are impossible to determine. God did not choose to include that information in Scripture. Still, doing our best to place the prophetic books in the proper historical setting can aid us in understanding them. The following offers three approaches to dating— by period/era, by century, and by range of years. Especially concerning range of years, authors of this book would not uniformly agree.

The pre-exilic prophets (Joel, Obadiah, Jonah, Amos, Hosea, Isaiah, Micah, Nahum, Habakkuk, and Zephaniah) prophesied before the kingdom of Judah was taken captive to Babylon. The exilic prophets (Jeremiah, Daniel, and Ezekiel) prophesied during the seventy years of Babylonian captivity. The post-exilic prophets (Haggai, Zechariah, and Malachi) prophesied after the faithful remnant of Jews returned from exile in Babylon. Please note that these groupings are not without controversy and the need for nuance. For example, Jeremiah began his ministry before the exile and could be called pre-exilic.

Some prefer to group the prophets according to the centuries in which they spoke and wrote. There are disagreements about this grouping as well.

- Ninth Century BC: Joel and Obadiah
- Eighth Century BC: Jonah, Amos, Hosea, Isaiah (who continued into the early seventh century), and Micah
- Seventh Century BC: Nahum, Habakkuk, Zephaniah, Jeremiah (who continued into the early sixth century), and Daniel (who continued into the latter half of the sixth century)
- Sixth Century BC: Ezekiel, Haggai, Zechariah

- Fifth Century BC: Malachi (who closed the Old Testament in about 425 BC)

The Prophets: Dates and Major Messages

Joel 850s To Judah: the day of the Lord (judgment) is coming.

Obadiah 830s To Edom: your Pride will cause God to destroy you.

Jonah 780–760 To Nineveh: repent or be destroyed

Amos 760–740 To Israel: your evil and oppression will be punished.

Hosea 760–740 Same basic message as Amos, very strongly stated.

Isaiah 740–690 To Judah: a worse fate than the destruction of Israel will be coming unless you repent.

Micah 735–700 He spoke to the rural people of Judah as Isaiah spoke in Jerusalem. Very similar message.

Nahum 650–615 To Nineveh: you will be destroyed —which happened in 612.

Habakkuk 650–615 To Judah: Do not lulled into complacency because Nineveh is no more.

Zephaniah 650–615 To Judah: the terrible and awesome day of the Lord is coming.

Jeremiah 627–585 To Judah: Babylon will invade and conquer you. You will be captive in Babylon for 70 years. Submit to God's judgment and you will live.

Daniel 606–536 Taken to Babylon in the first invasion, he was a prophet in the court of Nebuchadnezzar. Later he was in the court of Darius the Mede.

Ezekiel 593–571 Taken to Babylon in the second

invasion. Same message as Jeremiah in chapters 1–24. Also gave woes against the nations and promises of God's restoration.

Haggai 520s To the remnant who returned from captivity: finish rebuilding God's temple! Building began in 535; completed in 515.

Zechariah 520–518 God will judge sin and will send His Messiah.

Malachi 445–425 He condemned lax morals and faithless worship. He predicted the coming of John the Baptizer.

Separating the Prophets by Audience

Some prefer remembering the prophets according to the audiences that they addressed.

- Israel: Amos, Hosea
- Judah/Jerusalem: Joel, Isaiah, Micah, Habakkuk, Zephaniah, Jeremiah, Haggai, Zechariah, Malachi
- Jews in Babylon: Daniel, Ezekiel. Note: Daniel lived into the time of the Persian Empire.
- Other Nations: Obadiah (Edom), Jonah and Nahum (Nineveh of Assyria)

Questions for Discussion

1. In what ways might the designations Major Prophets and Minor Prophets be helpful to Bible students?
2. In what ways might those designations be misleading?
3. Why do most people think of prophets primarily as foretellers (predictors of future events)?
4. Why do predictive prophecies get far more attention than the moral and spiritual teachings of the prophets?
5. Why might some students advocate too strongly about the date that each of the minor prophets wrote?
6. For what reasons could the dates/settings of the ministries of the prophets matter?
7. Why would God have His prophets employ such surprising and diverse methods of teaching?

Endnotes

[1] Fee, Gordon D., and Douglas Stuart. "The Prophets: Enforcing the Covenant in Israel." Pages 187–211 in *How to Read the Bible for All It's Worth: A Guide to Understanding the Bible.* 4th ed. Grand Rapids: Zondervan, 2014.

[2] Duvall, J. Scott, and J. Daniel Hays, "Old Testa-

ment—Prophecy." Pages 435–464 in *Grasping God's Word: A Hands-On Approach to Reading, Interpreting, and Applying the Bible*. 4th ed. Grand Rapids: Zondervan Academic, 2020.

[3] Duvall and Hays, 438.

Resources for Further Study

Duvall, J. Scott, and J. Daniel Hays, "Old Testament— Prophecy." Pages 435–464 in *Grasping God's Word: A Hands-On Approach to Reading, Interpreting, and Applying the Bible*. 4th ed. Grand Rapids: Zondervan Academic, 2020.

Fee, Gordon D., and Douglas Stuart. "The Prophets: Enforcing the Covenant in Israel." Pages 187–211 in *How to Read the Bible for All It's Worth: A Guide to Understanding the Bible*. 4th ed. Grand Rapids: Zondervan, 2014.

Roper, Coy D. *The Minor Prophets 1: Hosea, Joel, and Amos*. Truth for Today Commentary. Searcy, AR: Resource Publications, 2012.

_____. *The Minor Prophets 2: Obadiah, Jonah, Micah, Nahum, Habakkuk, Zephaniah, and Haggai*. Truth for Today Commentary. Searcy, AR: Resource Publications, 2013.

_____. *The Minor Prophets 3: Zechariah and Malachi, The Intertestamental Period*. Truth for Today Commentary. Searcy, AR: Resource Publications. 2013.

Chapter 1

The Passionate Prophet

Hosea
Justin Guin

Main Idea

Hosea reminds you of God's steadfast and forgiving love for His people even though we are unfaithful.

Introduction

Prophets were often asked to do difficult things to illustrate God's message. Ezekiel ate a scroll as a test of obedience (Ezekiel 3:1ff). Isaiah walked around in the nude for three years as a sign for Egypt and Ethiopia (Isaiah 20:2–3). Jeremiah wore a yoke around his neck to illustrate the burden of the Babylonian captivity (Jeremiah 28:10). Their lives became a word picture for Israel to see as God sought to call them to repentance or pronounce judgment.

No prophet's life served as visual more than Hosea's. This extraordinary book of the Old Testament has some of the most startling illustrations to communicate God's message. His family teaches you lessons about God's relationship with His people. You learn about mercy, grace, unconditional love, and judgment. The Northern Kingdom's unfaithfulness both saddened and angered the Lord. Would He cast off Israel for their spiritual infidelity? While this outcome is what they deserved, the Lord forgave them and pursued them relentlessly. Hosea's name means "God is my salvation," fitting given the message of the collection of oracles that bear his name, which describes the steadfast love and salvation offered to unfaithful Ephraim.

Hosea at a Glance

Hosea is one of the eighth-century prophets, along with Amos, Micah, Isaiah, and Jonah. He is the only writing prophet raised in and ministered to Israel, referred to as "Ephraim." This was the largest tribe in Israel. The book's theme is God's unfailing love for Israel in the face of their spiritual infidelity. Even though Israel worshiped at the feet of idols and forsook the covenant made with the Lord (cf. Deuteronomy 6:4–5), the Lord loved them and sought to forgive them, restoring the covenant between them.

Political Background

Hosea prophesied during the reign of Jeroboam II (1:1, 2 Kings 14:23–29), and his ministry lasted about forty years (ca. 750-710 B.C.E). During this time, Israel enjoyed great prosperity that debauched them. Jeroboam

II restored the borders of Israel and was sent to be a deliverer for Samaria (cf. 2 Kings 14:25–27). He led three successful campaigns against the Syrians to free the Northern Kingdom from their yoke. Although God worked through him, Jeroboam was evil following the path of his namesake (14:23). After Jeroboam's death, Israel became unstable and fell further into spiritual decline under six kings spanning about 30 years (753–722 B.C.E.). Until this time, Israel was only threatened by weaker nations that surrounded them. However, Assyria gained power and threatened the nations in the Ancient Near East. Hosea named the Assyrians as God's arm of punishment and would carry Israel into captivity due to their apostasy (7:11; 11:5, 11; 12:1; 14:3).[1]

The Prophet's Family

The most well-known aspect of Hosea's message is how the Lord used his family to convey the prophet's message. In the opening verses, the Lord commanded Hosea to take a wife. Note Hosea 1:2,

> *When Yahweh first spoke through Hosea, Yahweh said to Hosea, "Go, take for yourself a wife of harlotry and have children of harlotry; for the land commits flagrant harlotry, forsaking Yahweh"* (LSB).

Hosea obeyed and married a woman named Gomer (1:3). The meaning of "harlotry" has been debated. Was Gomer a prostitute or a woman who committed adultery? Given the evidence in the book, the former seems to be the better option. However, you must not think of a prostitute in modern terms. She was a sexually immoral woman who was willing to receive gifts from her lovers for sexual favors (2:5).[2]

Hosea and Gomer's relationship becomes an illustration of that between the Lord's and Israel's. Gomer left her faithful, loving husband to go after other men who would give her what she desired (2:5). Despite her infidelity, the Lord commanded Hosea, *"Go again, love a woman who is loved by her companion and is an adulteress, even as Yahweh loves the sons of Israel, though they turn to other gods and love raisin cakes"* (Hosea 3:1, LSB). The prophet buys her back for fifteen shekels and some barley (3:2). Their relationship illustrates the steadfast love that the Lord had for Israel. God's people left the Lord and sought to worship in the fertility cults of Baal. Israel worshiped these idols because they believed the idols blessed them with things needed for survival. However, Israel didn't realize the Lord provided what they needed and was not a false god (2:8). Their breaking of the covenant equaled committing spiritual adultery by playing the harlot with other gods. When Israel returned, the Lord would accept and forgive them for their unfaithfulness (3:5). He had not forgotten the covenant as they did (2:13). Later, the Lord said,

How can I give you up, O Ephraim? How can I hand you over, O Israel? How can I make you like Admah? How can I treat you like Zeboiim? My heart recoils within me; my compassion grows warm and tender (Hosea 11:8, ESV).

Hosea's children were also used to convey the prophet's message to Israel. You are introduced to them in Hosea 1. His firstborn son was named "Jezreel" (1:4–5) and served as a symbol for the punishment for the blood shed by the house of Jehu in the valley of Jezreel. It is often understood this refers to the execution Jehu carried out to exterminate the house of Ahab (1:4–5). However, this position is problematic given the Lord commanded Jehu to carry this out as a means of punishment for Ahab's sinfulness (2 Kings 9:1–10, 10:30). A better option is to see "the house of Jehu" as a parallel statement for Israel. Jeroboam II was the last of the house of Jehu to rule the Northern Kingdom.[3] The valley of Jezreel was the site of many violent episodes in Israel's history. In this valley, Israel battled many enemies (Judges 4–7, 1 Samuel 29:1), Ahab murdered Naboth (1 Kings 21), and Ahab's family was executed (2 Kings 9:24–10:11).[4]

Hosea and Gomer's second child is mentioned in 1:6. The daughter would be named *Lo-ruhamah,* meaning "no mercy" (ESV). His third child, a son, was called *Lo-ammi,* which translates as "not my people" (1:9). Similarly, as does his first son, these two children illustrate God's judgment that would be meted upon Israel. They broke faith by worshiping idols, and they would face God's judgment. Israel sowed violence and would reap judgment. The message Hosea's children convey is a stark contrast to the illustration of his wife. Through his family, you see God's goodness and severity (Romans 11:22).

Religious Landscape

The failure of the priests caused many of the problems Hosea encountered during his ministry. The most well-known passage in this book is Hosea 4:6, and it is directed at their failures due to ignorance and the neglect of their religious duty to teach covenantal obligations. They forgot the Law, which had not been taught to the people. They suffered because of it. Worldly, ignorant leaders produced worldly, ignorant people.[5] Note this text:

> *My people are destroyed for lack of knowledge. Because you have rejected knowledge, I also will reject you from ministering as My priest. Since you have forgotten the law of your God, I Myself also will forget your children* (LSB).

Instead of consulting God's will and following His Law, they played the "harlot" by following pagan religious practices. These "teaching priests" would be judged for their lack of spiritual leadership (4:9–10).

Their lack of knowledge led to many sinful practices that took them away from the Lord. Notice some of the charges Hosea laid against them:[6]

1. Resorting to the high places where they loved to offer sacrifices to Baal (2:5–7, 4:10–13, 9:10, 10:1–2, 13:1–2).
2. Sexual relationships with cult prostitutes at shrines that profaned God's name (4:14; cf. Deuteronomy 23:17).

3. Open idolatry—they revered the calf images of Samaria (8:5, 13:2).
4. International intrigue—they see strength by aligning themselves with other nations.
5. Assyria (5:13)
6. Egypt (7:8–11)
7. Adopting international culture (12:1–7)
8. Israel trusted in riches/material goods instead of the Lord (10:13).

Thus, it is fitting the Lord said Israel was "destroyed" because of a lack of knowledge of God's Law. God wanted Israel to delight more in following His Word instead of Israel's vain attempts to worship Him through manmade practices (6:6).

Hosea for Today

Hosea has many faith-building lessons for the church today. Consider some of them to apply to everyday life.

1. God never stops loving His people even though we make sinful choices. The Hebrew word *chesed* occurs six times in Hosea. It is translated as "lovingkindness" (LSB) or "steadfast love" (ESV). It refers to God's faithfulness, grace, and mercy towards His people (2:19, 4:1, 6:6, 10:12, 12:6). God woos us with the gospel and desires faithfulness (2:14, 20). If we find ourselves

lost in sin, He desires for us to return to Him in repentance (14:2, 4).

2. We are destroyed because we lack knowledge of God's word (4:1–2, 6, 8–10). When we disown God's teaching, He also disowns us. Also, let this be a warning to those who accept teaching responsibilities in the church. Duane Garrett accurately wrote, "The preacher or teacher who sins in this way is not only responsible for his own misdeeds, but also of those whom he misled."[7] As goes the spiritual leadership, so goes the church.

3. If you sow sin, you will reap the consequences (4:11–12, 14; 7:8–11, 13–15). Hosea not only focuses on God's love but also emphasizes His judgment. Israel would face certain judgment due to their iniquity. Satan is still at work and takes pleasure in destroying your relationship with God. The New Testament writers warned about apostasy. Notice these passages in the New Testament: Hebrews 10:26–27, 2 Peter 2:20–22. Whenever you choose to serve pleasure and sin over God, you fall away from the living God.

4. Materialism is a form of idolatry that weakens our faith and diverts our focus. As noted in the introduction to Hosea, Ephraim had become a very affluent nation. Notice their attitude in 12:7–8. Does that attitude sound familiar? They were so consumed

that they thought they were above sin and could get away with immorality. However, God knew and would hold them accountable. Notice 12:9. Jesus promises that you cannot serve God and material wealth (Matthew 6:24). Paul warns about the spiritual dangers of materialism (1 Timothy 6:8–10).

Conclusion

Although it was written over 2,700 years ago, the book of Hosea has a relevant and powerful message for us. Many characteristics of Ephraim and American culture today are similar. God is still rich in mercy and loves you dearly! He pleads with you as he pleaded with the nation of Ephraim to come back to Him. Are you in a relationship with God?

Discussion Questions

1. What are some of the similarities between Israel and our culture today? How does Hosea help the church navigate these issues?
2. How does Hosea help us better understand God's steadfast love? What about His judgment? How do we balance these two concepts? (cf. Romans 11:22)
3. What are some barriers to learning and applying God's word?

4. What does Hosea 4:6–10 teach us about the importance of spiritual leadership?

Endnotes

[1] Jack P. Lewis, *The Minor Prophets* (Henderson,TN: Hester Publications, 1998), 26.

[2] Duane Garrett, *Hosea, Joel*, NAC 19A (Nashville: Broadman and Holman, 1997), 53.

[3] Robert I. Vazholz, "Hosea," *The ESV Study Bible* (Wheaton: Crossway Bibles, 2008), 1653.

[4] Garrett, 59.

[5] Warren Wiersbe, *Be Amazed* (Wheaton: Victor Books, 1996), 24.

[6] Lewis, 29.

[7] Garrett, 118.

Chapter 2

God of Locusts

Joel

Ed Gallagher

Focus Passage

Joel 1:13–2:2

One Main Thing

The Day of the Lord will bring blessing to God's people who recognize their own need for repentance.

Introduction

This past summer (2024) was a cicada summer. Such things happen every few years, but this one was especially intense because two sets of cicadas—both the thirteen-year and the seventeen-year varieties—hatched simultaneously. I'm not sure what sort of damage these bugs caused. The biggest problem they caused me was the incessant deafening hum that greeted any trek outside. I did not enjoy it, but perhaps I'm just a negative person. Bob Dylan took a more positive view of the noise when reflecting on an earlier infestation of cicadas: "The locusts sang and they were singing for me."[1]

Altogether different were the locust plagues that troubled the American Midwest during the 1870s. One such plague was immortalized by Laura Ingalls Wilder, who described her father's jubilation at the wonderful wheat crop about to be harvested, though it was not to be.

> Then Laura heard another sound, one big sound made of tiny nips and snips and gnawings.
>
> "The wheat!" Pa shouted. He dashed out the back door and ran toward the wheat field.
>
> The grasshoppers were eating. You could not hear one grasshopper eat, unless you listened very carefully while you held him and fed him grass. Millions and millions of grasshoppers were eating now. You could hear the millions of jaws biting and chewing.[2]

As Wilder recalls, the grasshoppers stayed for days, eating all the wheat and everything else, and laying their eggs in the ground, ensuring that there would be no wheat the next year either. This story concerns the Rocky Mountain Locust. The description above relates to the 1874 plague, and the next year would be even worse. Known as "Albert's Swarm," "the 1875 swarm that passed over North America had 3.5 trillion locusts, outnumbering the current human population on earth by a factor of 600 to 1."[3]

One can imagine the terror that witnesses of such a

swarm must have felt. The ancient Egyptians knew that terror:

> They covered the surface of the whole land, so that the land was black; and they ate all the plants in the land and all the fruit of the trees that the hail had left; nothing green was left, no tree, no plant in the field, in all the land of Egypt (Exodus 10:15).

The Bible represents God as sometimes using locusts to bring punishment, or perhaps a painful lesson in spiritual awareness. The prophet Joel used a recent locust plague to illustrate for the ancient Judeans their need for repentance.

Image 1 An illustration of the locust plague from the book of Exodus, image 80 of the Koberger Bible (1483), images available at the website of the Library of Congress, https://www.loc.gov/item/2021667062/

Image 1 An illustration of the locust plague from the book of Exodus, image 80 of the Koberger Bible (1483), images available at the website of the Library of Congress, https://www.loc.gov/item/2021667062/.

Going Deeper

Basic questions about the book of Joel are difficult to answer. We have no outside information about this prophet. Certain passages in this small collection of oracles fit best after the Babylonian exile in the sixth century BC, when it would be easier to imagine Judeans being sold as slaves to the Greeks (3:6). Joel's instruction to "beat your plowshares into swords" (3:10) seems like a later reference to an earlier prophecy giving the opposite counsel (Isaiah 2:4, Malachi 4:3). A post-exilic date for Joel, contemporary with Zerubbabel (late sixth century BC) or Ezra (mid-fifth century BC), would account for the focus on Judah (rather than Israel) at the end of the book (3:18–21).

Judah has recently been attacked by locusts (Joel 1:4), resembling an invading army (1:6). The locusts have destroyed the crops (1:10–12, 16–18) so that there is no opportunity for wine (1:5) or sacrifices deriving from produce (1:9). Joel interprets this locust plague as punishment from God for the sins of the Judeans, though he does not name any particular sins. In response, the Judeans should wake up (1:5), lament (1:8), and wail (1:11). Dressed in sackcloth, they need to fast and pray (1:14).

Chapter two warns of the coming of another invading army. This chapter does not mention locusts (at least, not until the promise of blessing at the end of the chapter, cf.

2:25), so are we to understand this army as an army of humans? Some scholars think so.[4] The description strikes me, though, as odd if describing humans: the invaders are "like warriors" and "like soldiers" (2:7); they are, indeed, "like a powerful army" (2:5). The similes indicate that Joel is describing something not human—probably another locust invasion.

Regardless of the composition of this army (humans or locusts), Joel identifies for us the general who is leading the troops.

> YHWH utters his voice
>> at the head of his army;
>> how vast is his host!
>> Numberless are those who obey his command.
> (Joel 2:11)

(To make it clear that the text refers to the proper Hebrew name of God, I use the English equivalent of the Hebrew letters, without vowels, YHWH, in place of the more common substitute "the LORD.") YHWH Himself is the one bringing this army against His people (cf. Jeremiah 25:9). Again, the coming threat should be seen as brought about by God because of His people's sin. These invasions represent recurrences of the Day of the LORD, the Day of YHWH (1:15, 2:1–2, 11)—the day when God acts to bring justice to the earth.[5] Whereas the Judeans no doubt longed for their God to act on their behalf, Joel's message warns his listeners to be careful what they wish for. The sinfulness of God's people means that judgment will be against them. "For the time has come for judgment to begin with the household of God" (1 Peter 4:17; cf. Amos 3:2).

In fact, the coming invasion is not so much punishment from God as an attempt by God to reform His people. He wants them to repent.

> Yet even now, says YHWH,
>> return to me with all your heart,
>> with fasting, with weeping, and with mourning;
>> rend your hearts and not your clothing.
>> Return to YHWH, your God,
>> for he is gracious and merciful,
>> slow to anger, and abounding in steadfast love,
>> and relents from punishing.
>> Who knows whether he will not turn and relent,
>> and leave a blessing behind him,
>> a grain offering and a drink offering
>> for YHWH, your God? (2:12–14)

This speech—echoing God's self-disclosure to Moses on the mountain (Exodus 34:6–7)—concludes with the prophet's hopeful surmise that God may show mercy after all. (The same "Who knows?!" is found also on the lips of the king of Nineveh in Jonah 3:9; and see 2 Samuel 12:22, Esther 4:14.) God even provides the words for the people to pray (Joel 2:17).

In the book of Joel, the Judeans make good on God's offer of repentance, and so the second chapter closes with a promise of prosperity (2:18–27). Rather than the sins of Judah separating them from God, now "You shall know that I am in the midst of Israel" (2:27). But wait, there's more! After the promise of near-term material prosperity, Joel announces the coming of another "great and terrible day of YHWH" (2:31)—great and terrible, perhaps, because of the grave consequences accompanying the response of people to what happens on that "day." For on that day, "everyone who calls on the name of YHWH shall be saved" (2:32), and so this impending day of YHWH entails the burden of choosing to call on that name. Those who choose poorly will be gathered in the valley of decision for an appointment with God on the final and terrifying day of YHWH (3:14), as Joel's final oracle describes.

Application

There is too much in this short book to explore all the points of application to the modern Christian life that Joel allows. Christians will be most familiar with the prophecy at the end of Joel 2 because the apostle Peter quoted the entire section at the start of his Pentecost sermon in Acts 2. Peter's interpretation: the day of YHWH prophesied at the end of Joel 2 has come; now is the time for choosing; now is the time when all who call on the name of the Lord will be saved (cf. Romans 10:13).

Joel also presents a wonderful illustration of God's mercy, of His patience with sinful people, of His desire to lead them toward repentance (cf. 1 Timothy 2:4). And our prophet tells us how to repent—rend your hearts and not your garments (Joel 2:15)!—a lesson we always need.

But here we will briefly consider the theme of the day of YHWH and what God's people expected from it. Joel does not have a monopoly on this theme. In the Minor Prophets, the day of YHWH is mentioned again in Amos, Obadiah, Zephaniah, and Malachi.[6] Especially Joel and Amos 5:18–20 give the impression that Judeans and Israelites longed for the day of God's judgment, when the Lord would straighten out the wrongs of the world and exalt the righteous while punishing the wicked. Both prophets mock their audience for maintaining such absurd confidence that God's coming justice would benefit them. On the contrary, Joel harangues his listeners about their own wickedness meriting the wrath of God.

Such a posture of the Judean people—trusting in their own righteousness while flummoxing at the sins of others—should be familiar to readers of the Sermon on the Mount. When Jesus mentioned the log and the speck (Matthew 7:3–5), He could have used Joel's audience as an example. Jesus's metaphor for sin relies on the silliness of the image: a log sticking out of someone's eye! Usually, a mere eyelash in someone's eye has them looking in the mirror or asking for help to get it out, and here's someone walking around with a log in his eye. Why doesn't he remove the log? He must not even realize it's there—which seems impossible; after all, it's a log. But Jesus's point is that, however silly and implausible it is for someone to lack self-awareness regarding such an enormous physical problem (a log in the eye), it is just as silly but very common for someone to lack self-awareness regarding enormous moral failures. (Think of the Pharisee and Publican in Luke 18:9–14.) A third-party observer can clearly see a person's faults, but that person remains blissfully ignorant of them. Such was the case for the Judeans in Joel's time; they needed a prophet to point out to them the logs in their eyes.

When Paul assures the Romans that "there is none righteous, no, not one" (Romans 3:10), and when he calls himself "the chief of sinners" (1 Timothy 1:15), and when Isaiah tells God's people that even their righteous deeds are filthy rags (Isaiah 64:6), we can be confident that we ourselves harbor sins, both conscious and unconscious. It is my eye that has the log. While this thought does not make us anxious for our own salvation—after all, there is no condemnation for those in Christ Jesus (Romans 8:1), not because of our sinlessness but because of God's mercy—it does promote in us both humility and the desire to grow in self-awareness. We need Jesus and His disciples (including the people we see at church) to point out to us the logs in our eyes and help us remove them. Fortunately, our Lord has left us the Sermon on the Mount and much other teaching, not to mention the Hebrew prophets, that reveal plenty of issues for us to work on.

Conclusion

The ancient Judeans listening to Joel longed for the Day of YHWH, confident that it would bring their salvation. Joel told them that for such a hope to become reality, the people needed to repent, and he told them how. The same lesson is needed in all ages for the people who claim to represent God in the world. And the promise that Joel told those ancient Judeans remains for God's people now:

the Lord will dwell among His people (Joel 2:27, 3:21; Matthew 28:20). With such assurance, we can reasonably long for the Day of the Lord. Maranatha!

Discussion Questions

1. Do you think the invading army in Joel 2 is a human army or an army of locusts?
2. Why do you think Joel represents God as leading this army against His own people (Joel 2:11)?
3. What sort of advice does Joel give the Judeans about how to repent? See 1:13–14, 2:12–17. Is any of this advice useful for Christians in the twenty-first century?
4. In what ways is the promise of Joel 2:28–32 fulfilled in Acts 2?
5. Why does Joel tell his audience to "beat your plowshares into swords" (3:10)? How does this command relate to the purposes of God in the church, or does it?

Endnotes

[1] Bob Dylan, "Day of the Locusts" (1970).

[2] Laura Ingalls Wilder, *On the Banks of Plum Creek* (New York: Harper & Row, 1937), ch. 25. For another literary depiction of a locust attack in another part of the world (China), see Pearl S. Buck, *The Good Earth* (New York: John Day, 1931), ch. 23.

[3] Jeffrey A. Lockwood, *Locust: The Devastating Rise and Mysterious Disappearance of the Insect that Shaped the American Frontier* (New York: Basic Books, 2004), 21. For a brief introduction, see Wikipedia: "Locust Plague of 1874"; Wikipedia: "Albert's Swarm." As Lockwood's book documents, the Rocky Mountain locust was extinct by the early twentieth century.

[4] Duane A. Garrett, *The Problem of the Old Testament: Hermeneutical, Schematic, and Theological Approaches* (Downers Grove, IL: IVP, 2020), 343–46.

[5] On the multiple "days of YHWH" in the book of Joel, see Garrett, *Problem of the Old Testament*, 348–49.

[6] See Amos 5:18, 20; Obadiah 15; Zephaniah 1:7, 14; Malachi 4:5; cf. Isaiah 13:6, 9; Ezekiel 13:5, 30:3.

Chapter 3

Amos

Andrew Phillips

Focus Passage

Amos 5:21–24 (New American Standard Bible)

> 21 I hate, I reject your festivals, nor do I delight in your solemn assemblies. 22 Even though you offer up to Me burnt offerings and your grain offerings, I will not accept them; and I will not even look at the peace offerings of your fatlings. 23 Take away from Me the noise of your songs; I will not even listen to the sound of your harps. 24 But let justice roll down like waters and righteousness like an ever-flowing stream.

One Main Thing

Our worship to God must flow from a life dedicated to living for Him.

Introduction

The term "Gnosticism" describes a collection of ideas about Christianity that began to spread during the late first century and early second century. It is an umbrella term that includes several different lines of thought, but one of those is a strong distinction between the flesh and spirit. The spirit was good and holy, but the flesh was evil.[1] This dichotomy allowed some to claim that what a person did in his physical body did not matter. After all, the physical body was evil anyway, and the spirit was the most important. Christians could do things physically without affecting the state of their spirits.

We are a long way from that time, but a similar temptation exists for Christians today. The focus is not so much on spirit vs. flesh but on Sunday vs. every other day of the week. Sunday is a day of worship, but during the other days, we can do whatever we need in order to succeed. We might be tempted to think that what happens in worship is isolated from what takes place in the rest of our lives. Someone could take unethical short-cuts at work (after all, that is just business) but feel fine after a Sunday morning worship service. A student might cheat on a test (after all, plenty of other students do worse things) and not give it another thought during Bible class. In this passage, Amos teaches us that this temptation is not new.

Amos was an eighth-century prophet who preached to the northern tribes of Israel. He preached during a time of prosperity, and he may even have been prosperous himself. The text seems to indicate that he has flocks of sheep. While there may have been general prosperity in the area, there were also many who were poor. Israel had not been following God's law, and they had been ignoring those in need. Amos pronounces a message to them that would have been shocking—surely God would not be angry with His own people? Earlier in this chapter, Amos named a few of Israel's sins—afflicting those who are righteous, taking bribes, and turning aside those in need. He depicts them running from the Day of the Lord, afraid of His judgment and searching for a place to hide. They might have thought they could find solace in their worship activity, but there was no chance.

Going Deeper

Israel knew how to worship. They took pride in it. There may even have been those who felt like they got a lot out of it. What they did in worship was not the issue; what they brought to it was. In this passage, God did not tell Israel He preferred a different kind of worship or that their worship activities were wrong. They were taking the right actions in worship, but they were not honoring God's law in their lives. Amos states that God is completely shutting Himself off from their worship—He will not look at their offerings, smell their sacrifices, or even listen to their songs. He names their religious acts, one by one: their feasts, their assemblies, their offerings, and their songs. God could not have been more definitive in saying He was repulsed by their worship. The term "your" is used repeatedly (*your* feasts, *your* assemblies);

they may have belonged to the Israelites, but they certainly were not the Lord's.

One of the strongest words in this passage, "hate," is used in Deuteronomy to describe how God felt about Canaanite idolatry, which included child sacrifice (Deuteronomy 12:31). Now it is a description of how He feels about the worship of His people. Earlier, in Amos 5:15, God instructed them to hate evil. Why would they need that reminder? Because Amos 5:10 reveals that they hated people who advocated for the truth. Their interests were exactly the opposite of God's. In fact, the next verse tells us that they were trampling on the poor and forcing them to give grain taxes while they lived in stone mansions. Israelite society had failed to live up to God's standards, and the wealthy did not seem to care. They ignored the poor during the week, and now God was ignoring their worship on the Sabbath.

Amos delivers a harsh word for Israel, but God does not leave them without instruction. Verse 24 gives them a strategy for restoring their faith and making their worship acceptable. "Let justice roll down like waters, and righteousness like an ever-flowing stream." One chapter earlier, God stated that He had withheld rain from Israel so that they lacked water. Yet that wasn't their only area of spiritual dryness – they needed a rushing river to wash over their brittle, atrophied faith.

They needed a stream of righteousness to cleanse their minds and hearts in the market. They needed a current of justice to crash into the city gates and change the way they saw others. They would have been familiar with wilderness "wadis," which would flow with water only during the rainy season and remain dry the rest of the year, but Amos's word picture is much different.[2] This stream of righteousness and justice had to be a never-ending flow in the lives of Israel. A momentary splash or downpour was not enough.

Righteousness and justice are closely related, almost synonyms. There are slight shades of meaning since it seems that "righteousness" places an emphasis on relationships in society, and "justice" focuses on establishing and preserving societal order.[3] Yet Israel had lost both of them. In Amos 6:12, Yahweh states that they have turned justice into poison and righteousness into wormwood, a plant known for its bitter taste. The sweet words of care and concern for others had turned into words of bitter bragging and rotten pride. The only way things could be changed was for the Israelites to inject faithfulness to God's character into their lives and community. Only then would the God who had withdrawn Himself respond to their worship.

Application

Israel knew how to worship, and so do we. We live under a different covenant than the Israelites, but the principle remains. If you have been a Christian for a while, you already know where to sit in worship, how to behave, when to sing, and how long to talk to people after the service has ended. In fact, we could probably go through all the correct motions of worship without even engaging our minds. In that case, it would simply become part of our Sunday routine, compartmentalized from the rest of life.

Avoiding that pitfall will require us to prepare for worship. That preparation will include taking the time for me to focus my mind as I enter the church building on Sunday. It will also include filling out expense reports honestly and accurately on Tuesday morning. It will require me to worship in spirit and in truth on Sunday, and it will also require me to treat the people around me with love and respect throughout the week. My actions during a worship assembly and my behavior outside it go hand in hand.

Conclusion

This is a tough passage to read but an important one to remember. Our critiques of worship today often have to do with subjects like song selection or sermon length. Yet God reminds us in this passage that worship is not only about our praise in the assembly but also about our lives in the community. We need to worship God in the way He has prescribed, and we also need to live our lives the way He commanded. We are called to be living sacrifices offered to God every day (Romans 12:2).

Discussion Questions

1. Think about comments or complaints you have heard before about worship. What do we usually talk about when we assess a

worship assembly? What qualities of worship are prioritized in this passage?

2. What are some reasons that we lose sight of important aspects of our worship? What can we do to maintain our focus?

3. How do you think the Israelites might have been tempted to justify their actions? How are we tempted to rationalize sin in our own lives?

4. In Martin Luther King Jr.'s "I Have a Dream" speech, he referred to the words of Amos when he said, "We will not be satisfied until justice rolls down like waters, and righteousness like a mighty stream."[4] Why do you think that phrasing resonated during the Civil Rights movement?

5. What are some specific ways we can hold onto God's righteousness and justice today?

Endnotes

[1] Jack Cottrell, *The Faith Once For All: Biblical Doctrine for Today* (Joplin. MO: College Press, 2002), 229–230.

[2] Douglas Stuart, *Hosea-Jonah,* Word Biblical Commentary (Nashville: Thomas Nelson, 1987), 355.

[3] David A. Hubbard, *Joel and Amos: An Introduction and Commentary.* Tyndale Old Testament Commentaries (Downers Grove: InterVarsity Press, 1989), 177.

[4] Npr.org/2010/01/18/122701268/i-have-a-dream-speech-in-its-entirety.

Chapter 4

Obadiah

Clay McFerrin

Focus Passage

> But you should not have gazed on the day of your
> brother in the day of his captivity; nor should you have
> rejoiced over the children of Judah in the day of their
> destruction; nor should you have spoken proudly in the
> day of distress. You should not have entered the gate of
> My people in the day of their calamity. Indeed, you
> should not have gazed on their affliction in the day of
> their calamity, nor laid hands on their substance in the
> day of their calamity (Obadiah 12–13).

One Main Thing

To please God, we should do no harm, and all the good
we can.

Introduction

A man was on his way from Jerusalem to Jericho when he was attacked by robbers. A passing priest saw what was happening and pulled out a blank scroll to record the incident. A Levite came along and took the man's wallet while everyone was distracted. Then a Pharisee passed by on the other side and congratulated himself for being such a good person compared to the robbers, the priest, and the Levite (and the victim). Which of the three proved to be a neighbor to the man who was attacked?

Obviously, the correct answer is "None of them." If Jesus's parable in Luke 10 had gone like this, the lawyer might have gone away thinking about the book of Obadiah.

Going Deeper

We can surmise that Obadiah was written in the aftermath of the 586 BC destruction of Jerusalem. It could have been authored by one of several Israelites named Obadiah; one good option is the Levite who had supervised the repair of the temple during the reign of Josiah, roughly 36 years before the Babylonian exile began (2 Chronicles 34:12). The shortest book of the Old Testament is primarily a promise of vengeance against the Edomites for their response to the suffering of the people of Judah. A simple outline might be: (1) God's plans to overthrow Edom (vv. 1–10); (2) Edom's mistreatment of Judah (vv. 11–14); (3) Edom's impending downfall and Judah's eventual restoration (vv. 15–21).

The conflict between the Israelites and the Edomites was foretold (Genesis 25:23) even before the births of their twin forefathers—Jacob and Esau themselves. Jacob fulfilled the meaning of his name ("supplanter," literally, "heel catcher") by swapping some food for Esau's birthright (Genesis 25:27–34) and then tricking their father Isaac into blessing him instead of Esau (Genesis 27). Though the brothers eventually reconciled to some extent (Genesis 33), their descendants often broke the peace.

Esau and his progeny settled in a mountainous region southeast of what would become Judah, extending from the Dead Sea to the eastern arm of the Red Sea, including Mount Seir. The Edomites did not allow the Israelites to pass through their land after the Exodus (Numbers 20:14–21). King Saul and King David later fought with and subdued the Edomites (1 Samuel 14:47, 2 Samuel 8:14, 1 Kings 11:14–17), but the Edomites eventually broke free of Israelite rule (2 Kings 8:20–22) just as Isaac had anticipated (Genesis 27:40). Thus, when Jerusalem was destroyed by the Babylonians and the people were carried away captive (2 Kings 25, 2 Chronicles 36), the typical Edomite was less than sympathetic.

Obadiah 11–14 describes a range of Edomite responses to the attack on Jerusalem. Some were onlookers, perhaps watching from a distance and saying, "Ha! Go ahead, Nebuchadnezzar, burn it down!" (cf. Psalm 137:7). You might have heard one say, "That would never happen to us; it is impossible to attack our cities and strongholds in the mountains" (cf. Obadiah 3). Other

Edomites were more involved, entering Jerusalem to see the ruins, looting possessions left behind by those taken captive, and maybe even claiming some parts of the city for themselves. Even worse, some Edomites who remained outside the city took it upon themselves to help the invading Babylonians round up the Jews who were trying to escape!

Other prophets agree with Obadiah's accusations. Edom "pursued his brother with the sword and cast off all pity; his anger tore perpetually, and he kept his wrath forever" (Amos 1:11). Esau's descendants "have had an ancient hatred and have shed the blood of the children of Israel by the power of the sword at the time of their calamity" (Ezekiel 35:5). None of these reactions was acceptable to God.

Edom believed himself safe from any repercussion because of his protected location, his wise men, and his mighty warriors, but Obadiah's vision declared otherwise. When God finished with the Edomites, they would wish that they had just been robbed by common thieves (v. 5)! Edom would suffer the inverse of the Golden Rule (v. 15) —what they had done would be done to them. Edom would be the dried-up leftovers of the harvest, and Judah would be the consuming fire (v. 18). Esau's descendants would be left with no wealth, no allies, no understanding, and no mighty men (vv. 6–9), and they would eventually be driven from their land (vv. 19–21).

Application

> *First they came for the Communists, and I did not speak
> out because I was not a Communist. Then they came
> for the Socialists, and I did not speak out because I was
> not a Socialist. Then they came for the trade unionists,
> and I did not speak out because I was not a trade union-
> ist. Then they came for the Jews, and I did not speak out
> because I was not a Jew. Then they came for me, and
> there was no one left to speak out for me.*
>
> — *Martin Niemöller (1892–1984), as
> cited by the Holocaust Memorial Day
> Trust*

For Niemöller, "they" were Nazis; for the Edomites, "they" were Babylonians. The question for us is, what will we do when "they" come for other people? When people suffer hardship or oppression—especially as a result of their ethnicity, political stances, economic status (whether high or low), or religion (or lack thereof)—will I say, "Oh, it's just *them*"? Will I secretly (or not-so-secretly) be glad that those people are finally getting what they deserve? After all, I am not one of them, which frequently means I disagree with them, which clearly proves they are in the wrong, and if they are in the wrong, maybe their misfortune is justice being served!

Well, of course, that is the wrong attitude and the wrong approach. If Obadiah were not clear enough on this point, we need look no further than Matthew 5:44:

"Love your enemies, bless those who curse you, do good to those who hate you, and pray for those who spitefully use you and persecute you." And if we do look further, we find Romans 12:20: "If your enemy is hungry, feed him; if he is thirsty, give him a drink." The tenor of the New Testament calls us to seek the good of others in fulfillment of the second-greatest commandment (Matthew 22:39–40).

One of the simplest examples of loving enemies is the tradition at sporting events that when one player is injured, all the other players take a knee until the player is able to return to play or leave the field. Until the player was injured, the players on the other team were his opponents, but when he faced an actual hardship, they were all rooting for him! Likewise, I may think my neighbor voted for the wrong candidate in the most recent election, but if somebody lobs a politically motivated brick into her living room, I ought to help her pick up the pieces and replace the window. When the guy who cut me off in traffic has a tire blowout, the spiritually mature response is to pull over and help him change the tire. If your meanest, most anti-Christian co-worker or customer has a medical emergency in your presence, your Christian duty is to help in any way you're able.

Conclusion

Obadiah is a small book with a strong message: Do not rejoice at the suffering of God's people. Ironically, God Himself was the true architect of Judah's punishment, but enacting justice was His prerogative, not Edom's.

Though the roles of Edom and Judah may be reversed when a faithful Christian observes somebody else's suffering, the principle holds true—if God takes "no pleasure in the death of the wicked" (Ezekiel 33:11), neither should we. Obadiah reminds us of the monumental challenge to love even those who hate us, in imitation of our Father's inimitable perfection.

Discussion Questions

1. When there are conflicts and other situations that we may be able to directly influence beyond "just" praying, how do we decide whether and how much to get involved? What if interfering may put us in danger? What if we don't have the training or equipment that would normally be considered necessary? What if the person to be helped is someone we've previously been opposed to? Considering the message of Obadiah, can we ever justify doing *nothing* as the right course of action, or are we always responsible for doing *something*?

2. What are some legitimate ways that we might try to protect ourselves against external threats? What are the dangers of excessively pursuing self-reliance (like the Edomites, and often Judah, did) instead of embracing our God-dependence?

3. Look up the history of Edom. How is God's justice demonstrated by the punishment of Judah compared to the fate of Edom?
4. In Obadiah, God promised to restore Israel after punishing them. How does that relate to your life? Was there a time when enduring the consequences of a bad decision ultimately strengthened your relationship with God?

Chapter 5

Jonah
Kaleb Baker

Introduction

I LOVE how movies often have a way of bringing stories to life for us. Each character often takes on a role that is relatable to us in some way. The Jonah narrative is a good example of this. There are several characters in this narrative that perhaps we can relate to or have been able to relate to at some point in our lives. Each of these characters is being sought out by the lead character in this narrative because the star of this movie is God, and He is chasing after the hearts of His people.

God

God is at the center of almost every story in Scripture. The Jonah narrative is no different. At the very center of each party's rebellion, God is ever-present. He is trying His absolute best to win each character over. He has a message for each person in this narrative. It is a message that is catered to the needs of each individual. The crazy thing about this narrative is that, at the heart of the matter, each person has the exact same need; it just looks different to some.

Jonah

The text tells us that Jonah was the son of Amittai. He was a prophet—a messenger of God during the reign of King Jeroboam II (793–753 BC). It was Jonah's God-given task to go to the people of Nineveh (modern-day Northern Iraq) and share a divine message with them. Jonah was reluctant to do so. He did not want to accept the mission.

Not only was Jonah a messenger of God, but he was also a devout Jew, an Israelite. He was part of God's chosen people, but I guess he had forgotten how special it is to be "chosen" by God. He did not think that the Ninevites deserved to hear the message that God had prepared for them, though God had specifically asked him to share it with them. Jonah decided to flee as far as he possibly could from the mission.

The Sailors

As Jonah plotted his rebellion, he bought a ticket and hopped aboard a ship to Tarshish. There is a little skepticism surrounding the exact location of Tarshish, but most agree that it is modern-day Spain. Noting the geographical location of Tarshish, you can deduce that Jonah was attempting to flee as far West as he possibly could from

Nineveh. When Jonah boarded the ship, he was met by the crew of the ship. These men were sailors by trade.

The book of Jonah depicts these men as "people of the world." Outsiders, if you will. This becomes evident when a storm broke out, and they began to pray to their god(s). Though this was not right, it was what they knew. I think this was commendable of these men and showed faith on their part. They begged their god(s) to deliver them from the storm.

Meanwhile, the one who knew YHWH was sound asleep in the middle of his rebellion. As Limburg puts it, "He can talk religion but does not seem to be much at practicing it."[1] This is an extremely convicting statement. Jonah knew God and knew what He was capable of, but he was trying to make sure that others did not. He thought they were undeserving of the message that God had prepared for them.

The Fish

Every great movie includes a climax. The climax of Jonah involves a fish from the sea. When the storm started raging, and the sailors began to panic, Jonah realized what was going on. He knew that the storm was a direct result of his rebellion. He knew that he had upset God, and so he told the sailors what had to happen. The only way to stop the storm would be to remove the problem from the boat. In this case, the problem was Jonah.

The sailors were reluctant at first, but Jonah convinced them that it was the only way. Almost instantly, as Jonah went overboard, a huge fish was there to swallow him. Jonah spent three days in the belly of that fish, contemplating life. I am sure that at the forefront of his mind stood the mission that God had laid before him. Jonah was given plenty of time to think.

When Jonah came to his senses and realized his mistake, he called out to God from the belly of the fish and petitioned God to save him. God heard the prayers of Jonah and delivered him. The fish spat Jonah out, and Jonah was then ready to adhere to the mission that was given to him. Jonah had received what my parents liked to call an "attitude adjustment." Or did he?

Nineveh

Nineveh was the capital city of Assyria. I'm sure this made it all the more intimidating to an Israelite. During Jonah's time, the city was just rising to power, yet it was still a highly influential and powerful city. At its peak, it stands as one of the most influential cities in Assyrian history. The prophet Nahum spoke very negatively about this city (Nahum 1:1–2:19).

Jonah's mission was to go to Nineveh and deliver to them a message that was personalized just for them. Perhaps some of Jonah's reluctance came from the fact that Nineveh was a wicked city. Perhaps more notable than that, Nineveh was an Assyrian city. For Israelites, this would have reminded them of the harm that the Assyrian Empire had inflicted upon them and their ancestors.[2] Nonetheless, Jonah was reluctant to go to Nineveh because he did not think the Ninevites were deserving of a message from God, much less a message of forgiveness.

The Sermon

After much reluctance, Jonah finally mustered up the courage to make the trip to Nineveh and share the message from God with them. The sermon that Jonah preached was a church member's dream. It consisted of eight words, "Forty days from now, Nineveh will be destroyed!" That's all Jonah could say, but as it turns out, it was all he needed to say. Nineveh repented and turned to God. God then changed His mind and withheld His wrath from them. As Nineveh was celebrating their second chance at life, Jonah was not so thrilled about it. Jonah got mad at the Lord for showing such a wicked city such great mercy.

Application

As we look at the Jonah narrative, it is easy to see that God was chasing after the hearts of His people. That is the role that He was playing in this narrative, the *chaser*. He chased after Jonah through the whole narrative. He chased after the sailors and won them over. Of course, you cannot leave out the city of Nineveh—the city that was at the heart of the mission from the beginning. There are lessons to be learned from each encounter with God in this narrative.

The Sailors' Encounter

Though it was only a short encounter with God, the sailors saw all they needed to see. It certainly was not part of the initial plan for Jonah to encounter these sailors. Had he just obeyed God and gone to Nineveh in the first place, these sailors would not have even been part of the narrative. They may have never encountered God. I'm not going to confidently say that Jonah's rebellion was part of God's initial plan because who would I be to try to predict the plans of an Almighty God, but if God wanted to work through Jonah in that way, He certainly could have. Nonetheless, we learn an important lesson from this encounter with God. God is working through our lives to chase after the hearts of His people. Even when we try to resist the mission, God will work through the resistance. He will do whatever it takes to win over the hearts of His creation.

Nineveh's Encounter

The wicked city of Nineveh's encounter with God was not quite as pleasant. In fact, it was quite terrifying. Despite Jonah's brief eight-word sermon, the Ninevites heard the message that God wanted them to hear. The text says, "They believed God's message" (3:5). They turned from their wicked ways. Even the king of Nineveh stepped down from his throne and humbled himself before God. Perhaps the lesson that we can draw from this encounter is that no one is too far gone to turn to God.

Jonah's Encounter

Though Jonah had already encountered God and knew God (or so he thought), I think Jonah encountered God in a whole new light. He learned that no matter how hard he tried, he could not run from a God-ordained mission. He learned that his judgment of someone or a group of people meant nothing. More importantly, he learned that no one was beyond God's grace and mercy. I think that these are valid lessons for us as well since we, too, are God's people.

Conclusion

As I read the Jonah narrative, I am reminded of a valuable lesson that Jesus taught during His earthly ministry. In John 8, Jesus encountered a woman who had been caught in the act of adultery. The Pharisees were the ones who brought the woman before the crowd. In their mind, she was beyond God's mercy, but Jesus said, "But let the one who has never sinned throw the first stone" (John 8:7 NLT). I think this lesson from Jesus is the same lesson that Jonah learned on that day in Nineveh.

In order for us to chase after the hearts of others, sometimes God has to chase after our hearts. No matter how hard he tried, Jonah could not flee God's persistence. As Christians, we often forget that all humans are created in God's image. Those who are not part of the Kingdom are no less created in God's image than we are. The only difference is we have encountered God, which means we have a message that has been entrusted to us. Will we share it or withhold it? How will we share it? God has shown us grace and mercy. Will we show grace and mercy to others?

Discussion Questions

1. Why would God pursue a prophet as unwilling as Jonah and a nation as evil as Assyria?
2. Do you think Jonah really believed that he could run from God? What must a person tell himself in order to believe that?
3. What seeds of faith should their encounter with Jonah have planted in the minds of the sailors who saw the storm calmed immediately?
4. How do you explain the effect of Jonah's preaching on the city of Nineveh?
5. What does the story of Jonah tell us about the power of God's message versus the power of the messenger who delivers it?
6. Why was Jonah so angry over the success of his mission to Nineveh?
7. How is it possible for anyone to remain unchanged by an encounter with God?

Endnotes

[1] James Limburg, *Hosea—Micah,* Interpretation (Louisville: John Knox Press, 1988), 145.

[2] L. Juliana M. Claassens, *Jonah: A Commentary*, OTL (Louisville: Westminster John Knox, 2024), 6.

Chapter 6

Micah

Ismael Berlanga

Focus Passage

Micah

One Main Thing

Which future will you choose? In the battle for His people's hearts, God offers us an alternative to living for ourselves by inviting us to His Mountain of Salvation.

Introduction

Micah can be experienced as a book of two realities competing for our hearts. On the one side is the status quo. In this reality, Micah paints a picture where truth is rejected, authority figures speak presumptuously, and trusted sources are bought with money. If we think about it, our world today is not so different than that of Micah's hearers.

On the other hand, God offers an alternative where the high places of power are judged and ultimately flattened. A new high and holy mountain would rise from the ashes and serve as a beacon of hope for all.

Going Deeper

Some may read Micah and ask, "Isn't the choice clear? Why wouldn't someone abandon a life of injustice and pursue a life of blessing with God?" Lest we be quick to judge, what hinders us from complete dedication to God? Are there high places in our lives that need tearing down? I invite you to begin thinking about these questions as we explore the book of Micah.

The Flattening

Power, regardless of its form, can freeze us in place. Power can also cause us to become indifferent to its corrosive tendencies. Who can withstand abusive high places when they seem too powerful to overcome? Micah's hearers must have asked such questions because his proclamation begins with the Lord of Hosts tearing down the high places of the earth. Micah says,

> Behold, the LORD is coming out of his place, and will come down and tread up on the high places of the earth ... mountains will melt under him, and the valleys will split open, like wax before the fire, like waters poured down a steep place" (Micah 1:3–4).

The prophet elaborates that the "time of disaster" will openly expose wrongdoers, and they will forever be known for their downfall (Micah 2:3–4). Because the power structures hurt the people instead of serving them, "Zion shall be plowed as a field; Jerusalem shall become a heap of ruins, and the mountain of the house a wooded height" (Micah 3:12). Out of the rubble, a glimmer of hope comes to view when Micah says, "I will surely assemble all of you, O Jacob; I will gather the remnant of Israel; I will set them together like sheep in a fold, like a flock in its pasture, a noisy multitude of men" (Micah 2:12). No matter how much power these high places wielded, none could withstand Almighty God.

Future of Hope

> It shall come to pass in the latter days that the mountain of the house of the LORD shall be established as the highest of the mountains, and it shall be lifted up above the hills; and peoples shall flow to it, and many nations shall come, and say: "Come, let us go up to the mountain of the LORD, to the house of the God of Jacob, that he may teach us his ways and that we may walk in his paths" (Micah 4:1–2).

The Mountain of Salvation, unbound by space and time, would come to be experienced throughout the generations. People would seek this holy high place out of a heart of desire and not by compulsion, drawing to its virtues. A shepherd of old would show the path to the Mountain of Salvation. Micah prophesies,

But you, O Bethlehem Ephrathah, who are too little to be among the clans of Judah, from you shall come forth for me one who is to be ruler in Israel, whose coming forth is from of old, from ancient days ... he shall stand and shepherd his flock in the strength of the LORD, in the majesty of the name of the LORD his God" (Micah 5:2,4). And again, "With what shall I come before the LORD, and bow myself before God on high? ... Shall I give my firstborn for my transgression, the fruit of my body for the sin of my soul?" (Micah 6:6–7).

Micah tells the people that the Lord's plan to restore hope ultimately involved a ruler and shepherd who would emulate the majesty of God's name. Who wouldn't want to follow a leader who was an extension of God Himself? There would be no comparison between the leadership of God's shepherd and the high places' abusive practices.

Finally, Micah's closing scene combines all these themes into one final case for God's path of hope. He says,

Shepherd your people with your staff, the flock of your inheritance, who dwell alone in a forest in the midst of a garden land; let them graze in Bashan and Gilead as in the days of old. As in the days when you came out of the land of Egypt, I will show them marvelous things ... Who is a God like you, pardoning iniquity and passing over transgression for the remnant of his inheritance? He does not retain his anger forever, because he delights in steadfast love. He will again have compassion on us; he will tread our iniquities underfoot. You will cast all our sins into the depths of the sea (Micah 7:14, 18–19).

What a compelling contrast between two realities! Not only would the Lord destroy the high places which had long led the people astray and inflicted pain, but the Lord Himself would shepherd the way. I invite you now to bridge the prophet's words with your life.

Application

A New Covenant-informed reading of Micah helps us understand that the Mountain of Salvation was ultimately the church, and the shepherd was Jesus Christ. This mountain became visible and accessible to all because it was spiritual in nature. Jesus, the "founder and perfecter of our faith" (Hebrews 11:2), led humanity to the great mountain, and the church still serves as a beacon of hope for the world!

That said, the battle for the hearts of God's people is not over. Whether you have been following the Lord for one day or a lifetime, you know that the spiritual battle for your heart takes place daily. Drawing from Micah's message, I want to share two observations that can help us in this daily battle. First, the Lord can still flatten high places that seem insurmountable. Second, He brings hope to our future when we experience life through Him.

High Places

In today's age of technology, busy schedules, and information overload, a high place will occasionally surface that will draw us to it. Said another way, the daily battle for our hearts and minds has replaced the literal high places of old but is still just as dangerous. Paul wrote,

> For though we walk in the flesh, we are not waging war according to the flesh. For the weapons of our warfare are not of the flesh but have divine power to destroy strongholds. We destroy arguments and every lofty opinion raised against the knowledge of God, and take every thought captive to obey Christ. (2 Corinthians 10:3–5)

As Paul noted here, high places still exist. Where they were once physical objects, they are now lofty opinions and strongholds of the flesh. They can draw us to their mountain so that we fall into their worship if we are not careful.

I invite you to reflect on the high places in your life. What draws the most time from you? What gives you the most meaning and purpose in your life? What poses the most significant challenge to seating the Lord as ruler of your life? Are there lofty opinions from others that challenge your self-worth? Are there strongholds that have proven difficult to tear down in your life? Though they may seem impossible to overthrow, all things are possible through the Lord.

Paul continues that every thought can become captive when our obedience to Christ is fulfilled (2

Corinthians 10:6). Through God's powerful working and direction, we can overcome the high places of our lives that have long plagued us. What is required of us is obedience to Him in all things.

A Future of Hope

If your life has been primarily one of your making, with little consultation or direction from the Lord, has it brought you fulfillment? I invite you to think about what you are lacking in your life. For some, love and acceptance are what they crave. For others, the lack of confession and forgiveness has led to stagnation. Each of us has unique needs that can only truly be met by our Creator.

Try as we might, no human construction will fill our Ecclesiastes 3:11 yearning for *olam*, or the Hebrew concept of the infinite. This yearning is for something that does not exist within the physical world. God placed this yearning within us so we would seek God's eternal nature. Pursuing God's infinite nature through the knowledge of Jesus Christ is the substance of the fulfilled life.

We find love, acceptance, redemption, purpose, and deeply meaningful connections on this sacred pilgrimage. The future of hope that the Lord offers does not seek to remove us from the world but to enrich our life experiences through full participation in the body of Christ. Jesus said, "The thief comes only to steal and kill and destroy. I came that they may have life and have it abundantly" (John 10:10). Life is God's gift to us, intended to be informed by Him, and meant to be an extension of Him in our physical world. Beginning in baptism and continuing through the rest of our lives (Galatians 2:20), our salvation and Savior continue to reconstruct our identity and all that is connected to it. The battle for our hearts is a life-long process of sanctification.

Conclusion

Where does the battle for your heart stand? Have you any high places that need to be flattened? Micah's invitation is to take full advantage of the Mountain of Salvation he prophesied about. No power is too great, and no high place is too powerful that it cannot be deconstructed and replaced for the glory of God. The choice has been placed before you. I am confident you have and will continue to choose the Lord! May the Lord bless you and keep you always!

Discussion Questions

1. Are there high places in your life that need to be addressed?
2. Has your relationship with God become stagnant? What stands in the way of new growth?
3. Sometimes, old structures must come down to make room for something better. What were some of the high places in your past? When the Lord replaced them in your life, how did the process of tearing down ultimately become a blessing to you?

Chapter 7

Nahum

Tim Martin

Focus Passages

Nahum 1:2–8, 3:18–19

One Main Thing

YHWH is the sole master over human history and all nations.

Introduction

The prophecy of Nahum stands with Jonah and Obadiah as the three Old Testament (OT) canonical prophets who did not specifically address Israel or Judah. Nahum and Jonah were God's spokesmen to Nineveh, the principal city of the Assyrian Empire while Obadiah prophesied against Edom. Unlike Jonah, which is primarily a narrative about the prophet himself, Nahum is comprised entirely of prophetic oracles of judgment upon the

Assyrian capital and the empire it represented. This is similar to Obadiah's prophecy against Edom. Oracles against ancient nations such as Egypt, Babylon, and Phoenicia are common throughout other OT prophetic writings. Assyria was YHWH's agent of judgment upon Israel earlier in the OT period. This fearsome and notoriously brutal empire fully conquered the Northern Kingdom in 722 following several years of domination where Samaria and her kings were little more than vassals of the Assyrian Empire.

Scholars continue to debate the time of Nahum's work, but many place his prophetic activity between the fall of the Egyptian city of Thebes in 663 BCE and the destruction of Nineveh by the Neo-Babylonians in 612 BCE.[1] Very little biographical information regarding Nahum himself is provided in the text, save a possible reference to his hometown of Elkosh in the opening verse. Even this reference is debated with some believing Elkosh to be an unknown geographical location while others propose it may have been the name of Nahum's clan. The book interestingly has a double title, "an oracle concerning Nineveh" and "the book of the vision of Nahum of Elkosh" (Nahum 1:1, ESV).

The date of composition for this book is also a source of discussion and speculation. Many experts conclude the present form of Nahum in the Masoretic Text (MT) is the product of a text primarily composed in the late seventh-century BCE combined with later post-exilic editorial work. The textual tradition for Nahum is relatively strong. In addition to the Masoretic Text, witnesses to Nahum from the Judean desert include scrolls found at Qumran, Wadi Murabaat, and Nahal Hever.[2] The oldest witness to Nahum is its Greek translation contained in the Septuagint (LXX) tradition.[3] Thomas Renz observes at times "the LXX may well preserve an older and better text" than the MT.[4]

Going Deeper

Nahum's message would have been shocking to the citizens of Nineveh and the Assyrian Empire but a comforting one for Judah. Judah had also experienced the hegemony of Assyria for nearly one hundred years, beginning in the days of Hezekiah (2 Kings 18:13–37). For the Judahite audience, the message of Nahum "dramatically portrays God overwhelming Assyria to relieve his oppressed people."[5] As Nahum persevered in the Jewish textual tradition, subsequent audiences reading his prophecy could also have gleaned valuable lessons from his message. Ehud Ben Zvi rightly comments,

> from the perspective of a readership well aware of the fall of Nineveh, such a fall from the pinnacle of glory and might becomes a paradigmatic example of the fate of the worldly, powerful oppressors and, above all, of the even greater power of the Lord who brings them down.[6]

This would have been a sobering reminder of YHWH's ability to bring ruin to those who oppose Him, pervert justice, and oppress righteousness. This would have been an all-too-familiar message to the people of

Israel and Judah, who experienced YHWH's fierce justice for the same infractions. For the original target audience of Nahum's oracles, "if there was any doubt that the Lord would take vengeance upon Nineveh, the evil capital of Assyria, Nahum with his graphic word pictures of her fall would remove it out of mind."[7]

The message of Nahum is centered on the sovereignty of YHWH, His nature, and the destructive nature of sin while also conveying hope for YHWH's people.[8] In Nahum 1:2–8, YHWH is portrayed as a divine warrior who cannot be overpowered or resisted.[9] His character is described as both a wrathful avenger on His adversaries and a savior for those who seek refuge in Him. Later in Nahum, these attributes are manifested in oracles about YHWH's vengeance on Nineveh juxtaposed by His mercy on Judah.[10] Nahum portrays YHWH as having absolute power over all of nature, able to dry up seas and rivers, make mountains quake, and tread upon the skies above them. Readers of Nahum in any age can be convinced of the Lord's absolute monarchy over creation and created beings. How assuring this must have been for the Jews who, save for a brief time during the Hasmoneans, were constantly under the rule of foreign powers such as the Persians, Romans, and the particularly oppressive regime of the Greeks under Antiochus Epiphanes IV.

At the end of these prophecies, Nahum provided a chilling and cryptic declaration directly aimed at the Assyrian king. Those whom he relied upon to guard his empire were asleep and this "lack of leadership meant the people would be scattered over the countryside with no one to assemble the people."[11] The political and military leadership under the king had become inattentive guardians who had slumbered while disaster had struck, causing an "incurable wound and fatal disease."[12] This chilling message would not have been unfamiliar to Nahum's Jewish readers. Many of Israel's prophets before Nahum had similarly indicted the leadership of Israel and Judah for their religious complacency and incompetence which led to the apostasy of YHWH's people.

Application

Modern readers of Nahum would also do well to recognize the power and dominion of YHWH over human history. Governments, people, and organizations who, by human measurement, possess incredible power do so only because YHWH permits them to exist (Romans 13:1). Often, Christians may get frustrated by a perceived lack of our Lord's intervention when injustice, oppression, hatred, and other unrighteous behavior run unabated through our society. We should remind ourselves just because YHWH does not act does not mean He is incapable of doing so. The whole of Scripture demonstrates our Lord is patient, and He also reassures us in the end, justice will be meted out on the unrighteous and unholy who reject the Truth of His Word and seek to hurt others.

Nahum's concluding oracle in 3:18–19 should serve as a potent reminder of today's Christian leadership. The members of the Lord's kingdom need strong and alert shepherds who cannot fall asleep at the proverbial wheel. Positions of authority within congregations should only be assumed by leaders who are committed to paying close heed to the flock and stand as watchmen dutifully scanning for wolves seeking to devour the sheep. Effective shepherds are the product of intentional and godly training which prepares qualified servants to protect the people of God. Scattered sheep are difficult to gather back together and are also easy prey for Satan's predators. These lost sheep, especially those young in the faith, are also easily drawn away and become lost, often finding themselves assimilated into flocks whose shepherds promote sin and worldly living.

Conclusion

In 2 Timothy 3:16–17, Paul instructed his long-time coworker how all Scripture was useful for training the "man of God." In context, Paul was referring to what we call the Old Testament. The prophets, especially those in the Book of the Twelve, are all too often neglected in Christian study. The prophetic writings have much more value than simply repositories of the rare messianic prophecies referring to the advent of Christ and the Church. They are, and will always be, valuable reading for students of God's Word. Understanding the ancient context and purpose of these writings can aid in sound exegesis and application for us and all generations to come until Christ returns.

Discussion Questions

1. E. W. Heaton describes the book of Nahum as having "very little spiritual significance."[13] Would you agree or disagree? Consider the reasons Nahum was considered canonical and valuable to post-exilic Israelites, Second Temple Jews, and early Christians.

2. Is it troubling for Christians that Nineveh's destruction would have been a source of joy and comfort for Judah? Should we not be praying for our enemies and those who persecute us?

3. Do we truly view God as the sovereign architect of human history who actively works on behalf of the hurting, weak, and needy and punishes those who are oppressing them, or was this theological perspective only valid for the ancient pre-Christian peoples of God?

4. YHWH used the Neo-Babylonians to punish Nineveh. Was the Lord's justice only accomplished via human agents during the OT period? What about in our current age?

Endnotes

[1] It is believed the prophet may have been referring to the fall of Thebes in Nahum 3:8.

[2] 4QpNah, Mur 88, and 8HevXIIgr, respectively.

[3] English translations follow the chapter and verse divisions of the LXX which has fifteen verses in the first chapter whereas the MT has only fourteen. Nahum 2:1 in the MT is 1:15 in the LXX and English translations. This variance has no real significance in manuscript studies since the chapter and verse divisions were not made in either the LXX or MT until the fourteenth–sixteenth centuries CE.

[4] Thomas Renz, *The Books of Nahum, Habakkuk, and Zephaniah,* NICOT (Grand Rapids: Eerdmans, 2021), 39.

[5] Kenneth L. Barker and Waylon Bailey, *Micah, Nahum, Habakkuk, Zephaniah,* NAC 20 (Nashville: B & H Publishing Group, 1998), 144.

[6] Ehud Ben Zvi, "Nahum," in *The Jewish Study Bible: Jewish Publication Society TANAKH Translation,* ed. Adele Berlin and Marc Zvi Brettler (New York: Oxford University Press, 2004), 1219.

[7] C. Hassell Bullock, *An Introduction to the Old Testament Prophetic Books* (Chicago: Moody Press, 1986), 215.

[8] Barker and Bailey, *Micah, Nahum, Habakkuk, Zephaniah,* 153–6.

[9] Julia M. O'Brien, "Nahum," in *The New Oxford Annotated Bible: New Revised Standard Version with the Apocrypha,* 5th ed., ed. Michael D. Coogan (New York: Oxford University Press, 2018), 1335.

[10] Bullock, *An Introduction to the Old Testament Prophetic Books,* 222.

[11] Barker and Bailey, *Micah, Nahum, Habakkuk, Zephaniah,* 241.

[12] Renz, *The Books of Nahum, Habakkuk, and Zephaniah,* 190.

[13] E. W. Heaton, *A Short Introduction to the Old Testament Prophets* (Oxford: Oneworld Publications, 1996), 17.

Chapter 8

Habakkuk

Zack Martin

Focus Passage

Habakkuk 1:2–4

One Main Thing

What do you do when your world crumbles? Aren't you a
Christian? Yes! You are a dedicated follower of God, yet
life is not fair. The wicked are prospering while you are
suffering. Where is God? Why is He not punishing evil?
How could this be a part of God's plan? My friend, you
are not alone. Habakkuk had these same questions. Let's
look at how God answered him.

Introduction

Habakkuk was a prophet who lived in Judah during a
very tumultuous time. It would not have been the best
time to be around because Judah was in a downward

spiral politically and spiritually. While it is possible to know the context in which Habakkuk lived, it is challenging to know much about Habakkuk himself. When studying the lives of the writing prophets, their biographical information is usually located in the first verse of the first chapter.

However, the book that bears Habakkuk's name gives us little information about him. Even the meaning of Habakkuk's name is uncertain. Some scholars believe that the root of his name means "to embrace" and that the Septuagint spelling of the name may derive from a root word meaning "plant or vegetable."[1] There is also some indication that Habakkuk's name is the same as that of a flower found in Assyria. What is conclusive is that it is a unique name that only occurs in this book.[2]

We can be sure Habakkuk was concerned with what was happening in the world around him. In the next section, we will pay more attention to the specifics of Judah at the time of Habakkuk, but knowing that he was a contemporary of Jeremiah gives us some insight. Jeremiah was a prophet known for his heart for his people, but his people did not have a heart for his or God's authority. Herbert Lockyer writes that a modern-day understanding of Habakkuk and his name may have initially created a prejudiced relationship. In other words, the people did not want an embrace from God.[3] They did not need a prophet to speak on their behalf because they were just fine living without God's authority influencing their lives. And why would they want God's rule over them? Life is "better" without it—or is it?

Going Deeper

For all of Israel's history, God had been battling for the heart of his people. God often did this through prophets and godly kings such as Hezekiah and Josiah. However, the reforms and restorations brought about by the prophets and kings did not last. For example, Josiah's legacy has a tinge of failure because he did not listen to God, which caused him to lose his life. Thereafter, the kingdom of Judah was in turmoil from within and without.

Enter in Habakkuk. Injustice was happening in the opening and on every corner. God's people had continued to stray in the face of God, and as a prophet, Habakkuk knew that God had always done all that was within His power to save His people. But this time was different. According to Habakkuk 1:2, God has been absent, and even when Habakkuk cried out, God continued to be silent. He was not coming to the rescue of His people. He was not battling for the heart of His people. What happened to the God who heard the cries of the Israelites in Egyptian bondage and sent Moses to deliver them (Exodus 3:7)?[4] For this reason, Habakkuk cries out, "How long?" (Habakkuk 1:2)

The violence that Habakkuk was experiencing must have been extraordinary since he mentioned it twice, but it was not as remarkable as the absence of God. Furthermore, God's absence in this situation seemed to result in His approval of Judah's current situation. Because a foreign nation is not mentioned until God's answer to the complaint in Habakkuk 1:6, violence and destruction must have come from within. So God's people would have turned their society upside down, and God was just "idly" standing by as if with approval (Habakkuk 1:3–4). Here was the heart of Habakkuk's complaint.

But God was battling for the heart of His people! God was listening! God did see the violence and destruction that were happening within Judah and how His righteous ones were being oppressed by the wicked. God gave His plan in His response to Habakkuk, found in Habakkuk 1:5–11. God was going to send the Babylonians to punish them.

Habakkuk was not happy with this news. He then had a second complaint (Habakkuk 1:12–2:1). This time, it was not about God's inaction but His action. Habakkuk did not understand how God could use such a people to punish His people. What a repulsive idea: how could a holy God use such an unholy people? God responded in Habakkuk 2:2–20 by saying that the wicked will not go unpunished.

So, in the end, God was listening! He did see, and He did act. In Habakkuk 3:8–15, Habakkuk described God as the coming warrior. He, indeed, was coming to save. The very thing that Habakkuk wanted God to do from the beginning of his cries, He was now doing (Habakkuk 3:13). Even though God did not act in the time and way that Habakkuk expected and wanted, God was always active and battling for the heart of His people. We should always praise Him for this very thing, even when we do not understand (Habakkuk 3:17–19).

Application

Keep the Faith

After Habakkuk's second complaint concerning the Babylonians taking action against Judah for their wickedness, God explained that Babylon was only an instrument of God's wrath, but that did not mean that they would go unpunished for their wickedness as well. But God gave hope to Habakkuk and those who follow Him. God told them in Habakkuk 2:4 that the way to survive the calamity that was about to fall on them was to remain faithful. Today, we must remember this as well. Similarly, Paul wrote that, if we trust (keep the faith) in the promise that "nothing can separate us from the love of God in Christ Jesus our Lord" (Romans 8:39), we will be able to make it through anything.

Be Silent

The Bible does not fault Habakkuk or any psalmists for bringing their complaints to God. Therefore, it is not wrong to bring our complaints to God. What is wrong is when we complain about God. However, an essential lesson for us is that when we bring complaints to God, we are silent before Him so that He can answer us. Furthermore, when God acts, He is sovereign, so everything He does is by His will and is just. So even though we may not understand it or agree with it, all we can do as creatures is to be silent because He is "neither absent nor inactive" (Habakkuk 2:20).[5]

Rejoice in All Circumstances

Habakkuk ended his book on a high note. He may still have been in the same physical predicament but was spiritually soaring. Habakkuk reminds us that, as faithful followers of God, we continue to trust that He is active and working, and because of who He is, He deserves our worship. In Habakkuk 3:17–19, Habakkuk has a severe list of economic disasters. Habakkuk is saying no matter what may happen to him, his family, and those around him, it will not stop him from praying. May we all be like Habakkuk! In the New Testament, the apostle Paul finds himself in prison and gives similar advice to the Philippians when he writes, "Rejoice in the Lord always; again, I will say, Rejoice." (Philippians 4:4). May we all be like Paul.

Conclusion

We will all experience times when we need to take our complaints to the Lord. But when we have done so, God will still call us to endure whatever circumstances life finds us in. We will do so in faith, knowing that God "never sleeps nor slumbers" (Psalm 121:4). He is always at work on our behalf. Let us endure, keep His commandments and faith in Christ Jesus, and worship Him as He deserves (Revelation 4:12).

Discussion Questions

1. In what ways are you like Habakkuk? In what ways are you different from Habakkuk? What changes can you make to be a better "complainer," "doubter," and a better listener?

2. Since God does not directly speak to us today, how do we know God's will?

3. In what ways does God battle for the heart of His people today?

4. What does Habakkuk teach us about the gospel?

Endnotes

[1] "Habakkuk," in *Holman Illustrated Bible Dictionary* edited by Chad Brand, Charles Draper, and Archie England (Nashville: Holman Bible Publishers, 2003), 696.

[2] Jack P. Lewis, *The Minor Prophets* (Henderson, TN: Hester Publications, 1998), 60.

[3] "Habakkuk," in *All the Men of the Bible* (Grand Rapids: Zondervan Publishing House, 1958), 130–131.

[4] S. D. Snyman, *Nahum, Habakkuk and Zephaniah,* Tyndale Old Testament Commentaries (Downers Grove, IL: Inter-Varsity Press, 2020), 57.

[5] S. D. Snyman, *Nahum, Habakkuk and Zephaniah,* 78–80.

Chapter 9

The Day of the Shoah

The Prophet Zephaniah's Call for Ruin
Jeremy Barrier

Summary

THE MOST SIGNIFICANT idea that emerges from Zephaniah is "The Day of the Lord." This idea of God's intervention into the affairs of humanity is striking. God's interest in the concerns of humanity is intense, and when the weak and the downcast suffer, God notices and acts. The "Day of the Lord" is *the day* when God will sit by no longer and will intervene for the sake of justice on the earth.

Focus passage

Zephaniah 1:7–2:3 (KJV)

> Hold thy peace at the presence of the Lord God: for the day of the Lord is at hand: for the Lord hath prepared a sacrifice, he hath bid his guests. And it shall come to pass in the day of the Lord's sacrifice, that I

will punish the princes, and the king's children, and all such as are clothed with strange apparel. In the same day also will I punish all those that leap on the threshold, which fill their masters' houses with violence and deceit. And it shall come to pass in that day, saith the Lord, that there shall be the noise of a cry from the fish gate, and an howling from the second, and a great crashing from the hills. Howl, ye inhabitants of Maktesh, for all the merchant people are cut down; all they that bear silver are cut off. And it shall come to pass at that time, that I will search Jerusalem with candles, and punish the men that are settled on their lees: that say in their heart, The Lord will not do good, neither will he do evil. Therefore their goods shall become a booty, and their houses a desolation: they shall also build houses, but not inhabit them; and they shall plant vineyards, but not drink the wine thereof. The great day of the Lord is near, it is near, and hasteth greatly, even the voice of the day of the Lord: the mighty man shall cry there bitterly. That day is a day of wrath, a day of trouble and distress, a day of wasteness and desolation, a day of darkness and gloominess, a day of clouds and thick darkness, a day of the trumpet and alarm against the fenced cities, and against the high towers. And I will bring distress upon men, that they shall walk like blind men, because they have sinned against the Lord: and their blood shall be poured out as dust, and their flesh as the dung. Neither their silver nor their gold shall be able to deliver them in the day of the Lord's wrath; but the whole land shall be devoured by the fire of his jealousy: for he shall make even a speedy riddance of all them that dwell in the land. Gather yourselves together, yea, gather together, O nation not desired; Before the decree bring forth, before the day pass as the chaff, before the fierce anger of the Lord come upon you, before the day of the Lord's anger come upon you. Seek ye the Lord, all ye meek of the earth, which have wrought his judgment; seek righteousness, seek meekness: it may be ye shall be hid in the day of the Lord's anger.

One Main Thing

When the "Day of the Lord" comes, it will be either a "day of ruin" (1:15) or "a day of festival" (3:18).

Introduction

One of my greatest pleasures is seeing the changes that occur in the Fall season. The beautiful shades of red, orange, and gold created by the reflection of the sun hitting the leaves as they begin to change and eventually fall to the ground. The month was October, and the leaves were in their full glory as I was on my way to the local Jewish synagogue in town. I was teaching *World Religions* as an adjunct professor for the University of North Alabama, and I had a special treat prepared for them: we were going to visit *Temple B'nai Israel* and hold an hour-long discussion with the Rabbi, who was waiting for us there. The most festive part of the year was drawing to a conclusion. The Jewish New Year, *Rosh Hashanah*, was just a few weeks ago. Yom Kippur (i.e., the *Day of Atonement*) had also just passed. Sukkot, that is, the *Festival of Booths,* had just ended, concluding with the high water mark for the local rabbi in the celebration called *Simchat Torah*, a day when the annual cycle of readings of the *Torah* comes to an end, and the great scrolls are often taken out and displayed. One of the special scrolls held at this particular synagogue actually survived the Holocaust, having come out of Europe to be preserved ultimately in my hometown. It was *supposed to be* an exciting time at the synagogue.

I arrived a few minutes before my students at the synagogue and was a little surprised to see a brand new, bulletproof door that had been installed in the building. This wouldn't have been all that peculiar if it weren't for the fact that there was also a police officer stationed in the parking lot as well. What was going on? You see, this was a week after the attack on Israel in October 2023, which, due to careful planning, had coincided with *Sinchat Torah*. After speaking to the Rabbi, I realized that even the synagogue in my hometown was receiving threats of violence to the point that the local police were stationing protection there 24 hours a day/7 days a week. I was shocked. This made me a bit nervous. As the students all began to arrive, I was watching intently as my one sole student with an Islamic faith—who also happened to have a home in Palestine—arrived for class. What was he thinking? My nerves began to subside as the Rabbi introduced herself, and the students seemed to be enjoying the lectures. We were about halfway through the lecture when my Palestinian student rose from his chair, turned toward the door, and walked out. Was he okay? I had no idea. The tension in the air was palpable. I honestly never imagined that my students who were trying to safely and objectively learn about the various religions around the globe would have to have such a direct encounter with the reality of the tensions that surround the various parts of the world where all is not well.

Going Deeper

One of the lesser-known festivals within Judaism takes place every year around the months of April and May. This festival is called *Yom Ha Sho*ah. It had already taken place on April 18, 2023, the same year of the events that I have recorded above. To be specific., this is a Jewish day of remembrance for what is often called the *Holocaust* or simply the Shoah (Hebrew, שׁוֹאָה), an event coinciding with World War II, in which more than 6 million Jews were exterminated. A terrible moment in Western civilization and the world! I mention it now because I quoted the passage from Zephaniah where this festival derives its name, Zephaniah 1:15, "... a day of wasteness and desolation ... ."

Zephaniah is famous for portraying the most impressive all-encompassing image of destruction and ruin that God will rain down on Judah, Israel, essentially all of the neighbors of Israel, and even as far as Assyria to the north and Nubia (i.e., Ethiopia) to the south. It is impressive. I have quoted only a fraction of this depressing "Day of the Lord."

The "Day of the Lord" not only serves as a reminder that God is not ignoring what happens here on this earth but that God cares. In fact, the "Day of the Lord" language becomes so complete and essential within the mind's eye of those who live and breathe the air of the land of Israel that this prophetic imagining becomes the core basis for the apocalyptic worldview that dominates not only the vision of John the Baptist but also Jesus Himself. As was once stated by the German Biblical scholar Ernst Käsemann, "The apocalyptic is the mother of all Christian theology ..." In essence, the idea of God's intervention into the cosmos to ensure that justice prevails on earth is *the theme* expressed so succinctly and beautifully by John's Gospel when we read:

> For God so loved the world, that he gave his only begotten Son, that whosoever believeth in him should not perish, but have everlasting life. For God sent not his Son into the world to condemn the world; but that the world through him might be saved (John 3:16–17).

The overarching theme here is focused on the justice *and* mercy of God. How can God have both at the same time? A dilemma solved through Jesus.

Application

I mention this and even allow myself the extension into the life of Jesus for one clear reason. Zephaniah is actually offering both in one: mercy and justice. The main reason I stopped my quotation of Zephaniah in chapter two, verse number 3, is due to the message of that last verse. I found this verse to be sitting at the fulcrum, the centerpiece, and the middle of the three chapters of Zephaniah, possibly for a clear reason. Read it again:

> Seek ye the Lord, *all ye meek of the earth*, which have wrought his judgment; seek righteousness, seek meekness: *it may be ye shall be hid in the day of the Lord's anger* [italics added].

Conclusion

Through the years of teaching Scripture to many different types of people in various situations with many different types of backgrounds, I have noticed one common thread amongst most people. They fear God! They are *actually afraid of God*, and when they read Zephaniah, let's just say that this doesn't give them more comfort. They know that ruin and destruction are real, and many people in third-world countries have seen it first hand. I am impressed by Zephaniah's call to humility. It just might be that Zephaniah's writings are more of an "Announcement of God's Sovereignty" than anything else. The *fear* that I see around the globe is actually a positive human quality that I have noticed. Maybe I should state it differently: not fear, but respect. A meekness and appreciation for who we are in reference to God, His sovereignty, and reign over the earth is real. While He does seek ways, through His Son, to offer me mercy, Zephaniah reminds us that justice must also be satisfied. God still hears the voice of those who cry out in their oppression. God hears.

While I can't pretend to be able to offer all of the

solutions for the problems and conflicts in the world, nor can I pretend to know how each global conflict will turn out, I do feel confident in asserting the idea set forth by Zephaniah as a solution to problems both now and eternally: "Seek ye the Lord, *all ye meek of the earth*, which have wrought his judgment; seek righteousness, seek meekness: *it may be ye shall be hid in the day of the Lord's anger.*"

Discussion Questions

1. What are some of the specific details of the "Day of the Lord" that are disturbing?

2. What do you think about Zephaniah 1:15 and the remembrance of the *Shoah* even in modern Judaism today?

3. What does a meek person look like? Do you know someone that you consider to be "meek" or "humble"?

4. Do you ever wish for God's intervention to bring about justice on the earth? Do you fear that day?

Chapter 10

Haggai

Baron Vander Maas

Introduction

I DO NOT TRAVEL by airplane much. Because of budget constraints and flexibility, I always choose to drive. However, I love to fly! I've never been afraid to fly, and, like a little kid, I love to get a window seat. If you have ever flown, you know that every flight begins with a safety briefing. One of the key features of the briefing is the requirement regarding oxygen masks. It usually goes like this: When an oxygen mask falls before you, be sure to put it on your face first before trying to help someone else put his on. This safety initiative is so popular that some even turn it into a metaphor for how we deal with other problems. Whether it's money issues, psychological issues, or work-related problems, the metaphor is a message to take care of yourself before you worry about others. While for airports, this is an essential safety concern, we must ask: Is it right in every situation? The book of Haggai opens our eyes to God's desire to be the priority in every believer's life. Haggai critiques the notion that our priority should be safety and comfort. The question that Haggai encourages us to ask is: What should our priority be?

Digging Deeper

Haggai is a post-exilic book dating sometime after 520 BCE. The remnant returned from Babylon with excitement and a green light from God and Persia to rebuild their holy sanctuary (Ezra 1:1–3). However, when the remnant got there, they lost track of their purpose, mission, and goal. The returnees delayed the building project of God's house but somehow found time to finish their own houses (Haggai 1:1–4). In God's eyes, they had forsaken the holiness of God for their own comfort and security; even though the people may have felt they had good reasons for rearranging their building schedule. By putting themselves first, they neglected God's commands.

The returnees' situation became even worse as God punished them.

> You have sown much, and harvested little. You eat, but you never have enough; you drink, but you never have your fill. You clothe yourselves, but no one is warm. And he who earns wages does so to put them into a bag with holes (Haggai 1:6).

It must have seemed odd that nothing they did ever

really came to fruition, nor did they ever find anything satisfying or satiating.[1] Their suffering was not a mishap; rather, it was a purposeful tool of God's instruction. YHWH seems malicious in this instance. What kind of God punishes His own people for the selfish reason of not building His house of worship? However, this was not maliciousness but judiciousness. God was keeping promises He made in the wilderness. These curses towards the people were most likely references to the book of Deuteronomy. God promised the children of Israel that, if they disobeyed His commands, punishment would follow. Notice the similarity between Haggai 1:10 and Deuteronomy 11:17, where God withheld rain in response to their disobedience. Another example is Deuteronomy 28:51: Moses previously described a nation coming to attack the people on behalf of God. When he spoke about what the nations would take away or burn, Moses used the same list of "grain, wine, and oil" as Haggai 1:11.[2] God will exact judgment on the people when they disobey His commands. This is not a depiction of God as vicious but rather displays an honest and forthright God keeping His promise to stand against disobedience.

However, there is good news. God's Spirit still was with them (Haggai 1:13; 2:4–5). God's critique is not absent from His correction and pedagogy. He is the Lord of Hosts who guides His people. God's presence is a sign of His unadulterated love and faithfulness to the people. In fact, His faithfulness shone in stark contrast to the returnees who foolishly ignored God's house (Haggai

2:1–5). But God was with them; rather than abandoning the people again, He taught them. Even in this confusing and foolish time of their life, they were given an opportunity to learn from their lack of understanding. Would they?

Application

I am always amazed by the smallest books of our Bible. While they are small, each of them packs a large punch. We love the big books such as Isaiah, Matthew, or Romans because they are large treatises of the Christian faith. But God's breath was given to Haggai, Obadiah, 2 and 3 John, and Philemon just as much as the larger books. We would be blessed to remember that. The powerful ideas that Haggai demonstrates are setting the right priorities and trusting in God's faithfulness.

The first is that we must get our priorities in order. In Stephen Covey's famous book, 7 *Habits of Highly Effective People*, the third habit is "keep the first things first."[3] Setting our priorities straight is difficult for individuals but possibly more so for churches. A thought-provoking question for leadership and men of the congregation: When leaders meet, what are the subjects and topics that take the most time? Is the spiritual health of the church analyzed, the evangelism examined, or the sick prayed for? Or are meetings covering only the "house" of the people? Are the meetings focused more on the physical house of the building rather than the spiritual house of the Lord's church? Haggai's directive was that physical houses were being prioritized over the spiritual house of God. Paul, in Galatians 6:7–8, puts it perfectly,

> Do not be deceived: God is not mocked, for whatever one sows, that will he also reap. For the one who sows to his own flesh will from the flesh reap corruption, but the one who sows to the Spirit will from the Spirit reap eternal life.

Whatever the church invests in, that is what the church is going to reap. In Haggai, when the remnant invested in their own houses, everything else fell apart. The church ought to be fearless, confident, and courageous, always trusting in the Lord. This is why we preach without falter, evangelize with zeal, and serve with compassion, because God blesses those who put Him first. Remember to "seek first the kingdom of God and his righteousness and all these things shall be added to you" (Matthew 6:33).

The second lesson of Haggai is God's trustworthiness; but for some, His faithfulness will be very scary. We constantly encourage one another with the words of Jesus: "Lo I am with you always" (Matthew 28:20). Jesus's presence is a source of comfort and peace in the darkness of our sad world. God is faithful to His people. God relishes the opportunity to prove and manifest His faithfulness. In fact, even Lamentations reminds us, "The steadfast love of the Lord never ceases, his mercies never come to an end; they are new every morning; great is your faithfulness" (Lamentations 3:22–23). All of these theological truths are encouragements in Christianity. The impact of these truths is on one central truth: God is a promise keeper! God is a God of justice and honesty. He will part the sheep from the goats, and no one is exempt from that final day of judgment. Haggai introduces us to a God who intentionally keeps His promises.

> You looked for much, and behold, it came to little. And when you brought it home, I blew it away. Why? declares the LORD of hosts. Because of my house that lies in ruins, while each of you busies himself with his own house. (Haggai 1:9)

The impact of this on the church is that God is not mocked (Galatians 6:7)! God will keep His promises of redemption and justice, He will be true in punishment, and He will always keep His word. This causes believers to realize that fear is the only respectable approach towards God. When we choose certain human priorities over spiritual priorities, God is true to exacting punishment for that decision. The wonderful, gracious, and trustworthy God we serve is true to His Word.

Conclusion

Priorities shift as people change. In fact, the only constant in life is change. So as we conclude our study of Haggai, one stance that should never change is God's place in our lives. God takes center stage in our decisions, our formation, and our desires. Yes, sometimes, life gets in the way. What seems to be more important in the moment takes our attention away and we flee God, not even knowing what we are doing. Haggai is a story of how God guides His people back to Himself. Through correction, the Israelites put God back on top of their priorities. Haggai is a story of God's faithfulness and pedagogy, in which God will not forsake His people. Rather, God will teach them to put the "first things first."

Discussion Questions

1. Write a list of 3–5 priorities we have in our lives. Now why are these our priorities and in what ways does God take priority over even these?

2. After reading Haggai, describe God's character. In what ways can we empathize with God? How do we relate to the returnees?

Endnotes

[1] "The people should have known something was wrong with crop failure and garments falling off emaciated bodies and not enough alcohol to drink away their problems." Robert L. Foster, *The Theology of the Books Haggai and Zechariah*, (Cambridge, England: Cambridge University Press, 2020), 25.

[2] Janet Tollington, *Tradition and Innovation in Haggai and Zechariah 1-8*, JSOT 150 (Sheffield: Sheffield Academic Press, 1993), 197. For more intertextual clues between Haggai and Deuteronomy see:

Michael R. Stead, *Haggai, Zechariah, and Malachi: Return and Restoration*, T&T Clark Study guides to the Old Testament (Edinburgh: T&T Clark, 2022), 25–26.

[3] Stephen Covey, *Seven Habits of Highly Effective People* (New York: Free Press, 1989).

Chapter 11

Zechariah

Bill Bagents

Focus Passage

> The Lord was very angry with your fathers. Therefore, say to them, Thus declares the Lord of hosts: Return to me, says the Lord of hosts, and I will return to you, says the Lord of hosts (Zechariah 1:2–3).

One Main Thing

The Lord is hard to leave; He has always battled for the hearts of His people. He continually offers us a way home.

Introduction

Zechariah is a post-exilic prophet. God's people had served the 70 years of captivity prophesied by Jeremiah (Jeremiah 25:11–12, 29:10). Their primary oppressor,

Babylon, had been dethroned by the Persians. A remnant had returned to Jerusalem. God had opened the door to a new future. Would His people walk through that door in faith? Would they embrace the joy and opportunity? Or would they repeat the faithless and hopeless patterns of the past?

Going Deeper

Zechariah's first paragraph is dark. God's people had embraced evil ways. They paid no attention to God's warnings. They fought the Lord and His prophets until they were overtaken—devastated—through conquest and exile. But their story didn't end there.

Hope permeates Zechariah's dark beginning. There's opportunity for return on multiple levels: return from captivity, return to God's favor, and return to joy. God still rules the earth and knows all its happenings (1:7–17). God still favors His people (1:18–21). Jerusalem will be repopulated (2:1–12). Faithful leaders will be raised by God (3:1–10). Through the might of God's Spirit, all humanity will be blessed through God's chosen nation (4:1–14).

The Lord blessed Zechariah to communicate joy and hope through a series of visions. If a picture can be worth a thousand words, what should we say of words that help us create pictures that we both see and feel? From chapters 2–6, we find a man with a measuring line reordering God's city, Israel regaining its status as the apple of God's eye, Satan being rebuked by the Lord Himself for accusing and attacking God's people, a stone with seven eyes that offers utter forgiveness, a golden lampstand symbolizing the light of God's word, a flying scroll bringing judgment on all evil, and four chariots which patrol the earth on God's behalf. It's as if there's no time to stop even to take a breath. God will be acting swiftly and dramatically. Prepare to be amazed!

God's temple will be rebuilt. God's people will be called "to entreat the favor of the Lord" (7:2). Before they can seek God's favor, they must be called to introspection (7:1–7). Are they just going through the motions of ritual religion, or are they offering their hearts to God in true worship? They must be called to "Render true judgments, show kindness, and mercy to one another" (7:9). They must embrace ethical and loving behavior (8:16–17). They must stop oppressing widows, orphans, strangers, and the poor (7:10). They must stop being like their fathers, who "made their hearts diamond-hard lest they should hear the law" (7:12).

If God's people would reject the terrible example of their ancestors and turn their hearts toward Him, amazing blessings would follow (8:1–23). Old people would live in safety listening to the joy of children at play, "marvelous" would be the word of the day, God would save them and make them a blessing (8:13), and many people would flow to them to seek God's favor. In short, Israel would be a light to the nations once more.

Zechariah 9 offers a major change in tone. It's as if the Lord anticipates a major challenge that His people will face as they contemplate the joys presented in chapters 1–7. "What of our enemies? We live at the crossroads of empires. We face fearsome enemies on every side."

God offers three answers through His prophet. The first is confirmation that God sees the dangers. Second is reassurance that the Lord will deal with each enemy (9:4, 6, 8). Third, and most important, the Lord will be sending a King, "just and having salvation, lowly, and riding on a colt, the foal of a donkey" (9:9). God has dealt with and can deal with human empires, but the GREAT wonder of God is His ultimate defeat of Satan and sin through the sacrifice of His Son!

The latter chapters of Zechariah employ apocalyptic imagery. In judgment God will use arrows like lightning and whirlwinds (9:14). The mightiest of nations will be brought down (10:11). God will allow false leaders to deceive the evil (11:1–17). The Lord will afford the faithful inhabitants of Jerusalem amazing protection, but those who oppose Him will mourn with unimaginable sorrow (12:1–13:9). A fierce and terrible day of the Lord is coming (14:1–15). But in the end, the King, the Lord of hosts, will be worshiped and adored. There is no defeat for God and no ultimate defeat for His people, those who follow Him in righteousness.

Application

In this sin-damaged world, people are often slow to make the first move toward forgiveness and reconciliation. God, who is sinless and without fault, has been making the first move since creation. He came to Adam and Eve in the garden after they sinned (Genesis 3). He came to Cain even before he sinned and then again afterward (Genesis 4). Through His prophets, He came to Israel with words of warning and offers of forgiveness countless times. None of those offers is clearer than Zechariah's message of hope. In our age, God always has an offer of love, hope, and forgiveness through Jesus (John 3:16–17, Romans 5:6–11). His goodness and character never change.

Fatalism is not a Biblical doctrine. No one is doomed by his parentage or her past. From Ezekiel 18 to the examples of Rahab (Joshua 2), David (Psalm 51), those who helped kill Jesus (Acts 2:23 & 36–39), Saul of Tarsus (Acts 26:9–18), and some of the Christians in Corinth (1 Corinthians 6:9–11), we see that Zechariah is not alone in offering hope and joy to all who would repent and choose to love God. The actions of others cannot doom us.

As much as Zechariah affirms God's mercy and grace, he also reminds us that the Lord never compromises with evil. He never relaxes His standard of holiness and obedience. God's chosen people will be judged when they embrace evil ways (Zechariah 1:4–6). Those who harm His people will be judged (Zechariah 2). Even nations that rebel against God will be judged (Zechariah 9). God holds each of us accountable for our words and actions.

God delights in blessing His people (Zechariah 2:10–12). Throughout history, He has loved to dwell with His faithful people (Psalm 15 & 24). The same will be true when Jesus comes to take us home forever (Revelation 21:1–4). God works so hard to make us fit to dwell with Him!

God's blessings are myriad and majestic. Zechariah reminds us that those blessings include the offer to return to God when we sin (1:3, 8:14–15), reminders of the cost of rebellion (1:4–6, 5:1–4), reminders that God is all-knowing (1:7–11, 6:1–8), reminders of His amazing mercy (1:13–17, 10:6–12), reminders that we must practice mercy and justice (7:8–10, 8:16–17), reminders that God's patience with the rebellious has limits (7:11–14), and reminders that the King of Kings is coming (9:9–10, 12:10, 13:7–9, perhaps 11:12–13). From the perspective of Zechariah, that final reminder spoke of Jesus's first coming. From our perspective, we look forward to His final return.

Conclusion

Zechariah is a challenging book. That helps explain why it is often neglected in our study. We're wise to recognize the blessings of a healthy challenge. Particularly with the apocalyptic chapters, certainty of understanding on every point may be beyond us. Even that can bless us with deeper humility and appreciation for the mysteries of God. The main message of Zechariah, however, is beautifully clear. Regardless of our histories, God still loves us and wants us to love Him. He continually encourages us to come home.

Discussion Questions

1. Why is Zechariah so blunt with his people about the terrible conduct of their ancestors? How could that realization help them?

2. Zechariah's offer of hope to his people strongly supports the truth of Ezekiel 18. Having rebellious parents does not doom their children to repeat that pattern. Why do some people have such difficulty believing this truth?

3. Visit Zechariah 1:3 again. Three times in one short verse we read "declares the Lord" or "says the Lord." Why such strong emphasis on the fact that this message is from the Lord?

4. Of all the encouraging visions within the book of Zechariah, which do you find most impressive? Why?

5. Why does the prophet give such strong emphasis to basic kindness, justice, and mercy (7:8–10, 8:16–17)?

6. In what ways are the three clearly Messianic references in Zechariah (9:9–10, 12:10, 13:7–9) a blessing to our faith? Why would the Holy Spirit include such references?

7. In what ways does the book of Zechariah remind us that God cares about our hearts (motive, love, intent) as we offer Him worship and service? See 7:4–7 & 8:18–19.

Chapter 12

Malachi

Todd Johnston

Focus Passage

MALACHI 1:1–14, 3:6–18

One Main Thing

God has loved and chosen us. We must ensure that, in all ways, we love and choose Him.

Introduction

Who holds your heart? In counseling, the practice of examining your principles, values, and morals not only helps to define who you are but also helps paint a picture of where your true desires lie. It seems there are a few things in common when it comes to what practices define and inform someone's priorities. A preacher told me once that the acronym for percentage is PCT, and 100 *pct* of who we are and what we do is seen through the People we are surrounded by, the Circumstances we are found in, and the Things we have. In other words, our relationships, time, and where we spend our money are true indicators of what or who holds our hearts.

The apostle Paul says we are crucified with Christ; therefore, we no longer live for ourselves, but Christ lives in and through us (Galatians 2:20). This emphatically implies that our lives are no longer our own. Our relationships, time, money, and all things belong to God. This requires complete and utter faithfulness. Malachi expresses God's call for faithfulness. The people have lost their focus on the importance of their covenant relationship, true and acceptable worship, and generosity that is after all, the greatest command is to love God with all we have and the second is to love others as ourselves (Matthew 22:37–39).

Going Deeper

Malachi tells the story of a conversation between God and His people. Malachi was written during the post-exilic period. The people have returned home, but their hearts have not returned to righteousness. In four short chapters, God outlines six issues with the behavior of His people which have distanced them from His righteousness and holy standard. The people, unfortunately, are more like the world and less like their God.

1. In Malachi 1:1–5, God through Malachi expresses His complete love for the people. He reminds them that He has never

abandoned them although they, through their behaviors, have abandoned God. However, despite their failures, God remains faithful.

2. Malachi 1:6–2:9 presents the second dispute. God brings attention to the polluted and irreverent worship of the people. The Israelites are offering blemished sacrifices—reminiscent of the unacceptable offerings of Cain all the way back in the early pages of Genesis. These actions illuminate the heart of the people. Jesus will later tell the Pharisees, "This people honors me with their lips, but their heart is far from me" (Matthew 15:8). It seems the message is not so different hundreds of years earlier.

3. In chapter 2:10–16, Malachi addresses the unfaithfulness of the people. Not so different than their ancestors before the exile, the people were giving themselves over into idolatrous practices. They have abandoned their wives and their God.

4. We see the people complain and accuse God of neglecting them in chapter 2:17–3:5. God responds with a promise to send a messenger before Himself and eventually bring about purification. This passage seems to allude to the coming of John the Baptist (Mark 1:2–4), who prepares the way for Jesus's ultimate arrival. There will be a reckoning to restore righteous order among the people of the Lord.

5. The fifth dispute is found in Malachi 3:6–12. Here, we see God accusing the people of robbing Him through a failure to properly tithe. The people had neglected to tithe but had no issue spending their money in unholy ways. The issue here is not about money. This is about trust and commitment. Is God trusted enough to give generously and willingly? Is the commitment of the people strong enough to rightfully acknowledge that all we have belongs to God? To whom do our hearts belong?

6. Lastly, in chapter 3:13–18, the people complain about how honest God has been. Ultimately, they are upset that God has acknowledged their wrongs. Doesn't seem right, does it? God's response is to share a powerful message. There will be a Day of the Lord when God will bring His final judgment. The unrighteous will fear this day, yet the faithful remnant will find hope and redemption on this day. What is destruction to one is deliverance to another.

The final chapter, just six verses long, dives deeper into the Day of the Lord. This is a common theme throughout the prophetic writings. A day of judgment for the unrighteous and a day of deliverance for those called according to His purpose. God challenges His people to remember the law and look forward to the coming of the Messiah. The book is profound yet simple. The people have fallen victim to the sinful nature of the world. They have been plucked from the proverbial forbidden tree. With their relationships, time, and money, they have neglected God, and their heart is far from Him. Malachi is, as much as any other, a book filled with a call rooted in grace and angst. Abandon the world and follow the Word. God loves us. God chooses us. Love and choose Him back.

Application

The minor prophets, while written to a people existing long before today, have powerful messages for all people of all times. Malachi is no different. One would think that a people returning from exile would be thankful and responsible with their call to belong to the one true God. However, not so different than those who came before, and those who would come after, the people find themselves in vain worship, faithless, greedy, and losing hope in their current condition. It's in what's missing that we find the main four lessons from Malachi.

Worship: We can be hard on the Israelites at times and for the right reasons. Their sacrifices were blemished, and their focus was on cutting corners, hasty practice, and cheating God. What about our worship today? God desires our full attention and devotion. Our desire must be fully on praising and glorifying the Father every chance we get with all we have. We certainly ought to give God our best and not the rest.

Faithfulness: Malachi focuses often on covenant relationships. Our relationships, especially marriage, reflect our relationship with God (Ephesians 5:32). Therefore, we have an obligation to reflect God's love and truth in how we treat others. In a world that seems to diminish the value of commitment and love, we must shine as lights of hope. This means we humble ourselves and have the sacrificial mind of Christ (Philippians 2:1–11). Instead of promoting ourselves and our own self-interests, we promote others. To be selfless, we must think of our self-less.

Generosity: Generosity is not about how much we give but about *how* we give. It's all about the heart behind the giver. The problem the Israelites were having was one of greed, selfishness, and just a lack of giving at all. They were neglecting to give back to the one who had given them all they had. This seems to be an issue of trust. God challenges the people and reminds them that when they give, He will give back more than they could ever ask for. God always has and always will take care of His people. Jesus makes this clear in the Sermon on the Mount (Matthew 6:19–34).

Hope: The book of Malachi ends with a call of hope for the righteous. In a world filled with brokenness, hope is exactly what the people need. It's exactly what we need today. This hope was presented in the promise of the "Day of the Lord," and that promise still exists for us today. We await the day of the Lord's return to call us home. As we wait, we anchor our hope in the love, faithfulness, and generosity that God has already shown us.

Conclusion

Malachi, the last chapter of the Old Testament, is a prophecy calling the people to turn their hearts back to God. Their worship was in vain, their relationships were wrecked, they were greedy, and many had lost hope due to their own negative behavior. Yet, God had never left or forsaken them. God desires full devotion and sacrifice, commands commitment in our covenantal relationships, requires purposeful generosity, and provides hope to all who righteously live according to His will. Hope is still alive for those whose heart belongs to God.

God has loved and chosen us. We must ensure that in all ways we love and choose Him. God is battling for our hearts. So, to whom does your heart belong? Think about where our time, money, and resources are spent. Think about the people, circumstances, and things we surround ourselves with. If all these things are not pointed toward God, then does our heart belong to Him? God is battling for our hearts, but the battle should not be too hard. We will all do well to respond to the call of God with humility, repentance, and devotion.

Discussion Questions

1. What does Malachi teach us in the church about the purpose and posture of worship?
2. Malachi critiques the priesthood, the spiritual leadership. What responsibility do

our spiritual leaders in the church have today?

3. In what ways does Malachi's teaching about tithing help us to understand our connection to giving and stewardship?

4. What are some modern ways in which we have "lost our first love"?

5. Is the "Day of the Lord" still relevant, and does it comfort us or terrify us?

Chapter 13

Malachi

Wayne Kilpatrick

Focus Text

MALACHI

One Main Thing

This book is an oracle or strong message from Jehovah to His people Israel, relayed to them by Malachi, whose name is significant—"My Messenger." The LXX has "Malachias" as the title of his book. "Malachias"—"the messenger of Jehovah." It is he who proclaims his office and delivers the message from God to Israel.

Introduction

The message is composed of rebuking and threatening, brought on by the controversy God has with Israel's priests and its people. The message contains a promise of comfort and hope. The entire oracle reveals God's love for His people if they will turn back and follow His laws. God's proof of His love, if the people demand it, can be found in the contrast between their own history and the history of Edom. Edom was a brother nation through Esau. From twin brothers, sons of Isaac and of Abraham, Israel and Edom sprang. Israel's history, though brief, is yet summarized as "I loved Jacob," whereas on Esau's heritage, look at the desolation and ruin of his country and the hopeless failure of his efforts to return and restore (as Israel had done after his captivity in Babylon). The everlasting sentence of irrevocable doom, "I hated Esau," is eternally inscribed upon the pages of time.

On the one hand, there is a nation in perpetual desolation which proves that the wrath of God rests upon it. It is thus referred to as "the border of wickedness." On the other hand, Israel is called "safe beneath the shelter of the Almighty," and they watched from afar the perpetual desolation of Esau's heritage. Malachi gave a strong warning to all of Israel by reminding them what happened to Edom. An echo from what Amos wrote, "You only have I known of all the families of the earth: therefore, I will punish you for all your iniquities." (Amos 3:2 KJV).

The book contains only four chapters, yet these chapters are filled with lessons for Israel and all generations that followed. There are seven times that Israel challenged God on something God accused them of doing or not doing. One time they challenged God on what He said He did. Malachi ends his message with a promise of hope for those who will return to the Lord and His laws.

He also leaves a stern warning for those who refuse to return to the Lord.

Going Deeper

After making himself known and that his authority for the message was from God, Malachi immediately pointed a finger at the priests:

> I have loved you, saith the LORD. Yet ye say, *Wherein hast thou loved us?* Was not Esau Jacob's brother? saith the LORD: yet I loved Jacob (Malachi 1:2).

How can men in a leadership role over God's people ask God such a question as that? God reminded them of His protective grace in the way He dealt with their nation as opposed to Esau's nation. (1:2–3). Israel was still there as opposed to Edom's perpetual desolation. That was proof enough as far as God was concerned. This was the only time in Malachi's book that the priests challenged God as to what He said He had done. Hereafter, the priests and people were challenging God as to what He accused them of doing or not doing.

First Accusation Challenged

> A son honors his father, and a servant his master: if then I be a father, where is mine honor? And if I be a master, where is my fear? saith the LORD of hosts unto you, O priests, that despise my name. And ye say, Wherein have we despised thy name? (Malachi 1:6)

God pointed out He is a father and a master. Where was the honor that was deservedly His? They failed to honor their heavenly Father. He then pointed out how they failed to honor and fear Him.

Second Accusation Challenged

> Ye offer polluted bread upon mine altar; and ye say, *Wherein have we polluted thee?* In that ye say, The table of the LORD is contemptible. And if ye offer the blind for sacrifice, is it not evil? and if ye offer the lame and sick, is it not evil? offer it now unto thy governor; will he be pleased with thee or accept thy person? saith the LORD of hosts. (Malachi 1:7–8)

God reminded the priests that they would not offer such sacrifices to earthly governors, and yet they dared offer such to God who rules over all earthly magistrates. The way the priests offered such corrupt sacrifices also showed disrespect and a lack of godly fear toward the heavenly Father. The priests were the reason the people of Israel were in such poor spiritual condition. Malachi challenged the priests to seek proof by offering such offerings to God and see if God would answer their requests.

> And now, I pray you, beseech God that he will be gracious unto us: this hath been by your means: will he regard your persons? saith the LORD of hosts (Malachi 1:9).

The answer is emphatically NO. Malachi told the

sad tale of how the polluted sacrifices would come back on the heads of the ones who made such offerings as a curse.

> But cursed be the deceiver, which hath in his flock a male, and vows, and sacrifices unto the Lord a corrupt thing: for I am a great King, saith the LORD of hosts, and my name is dreadful among the heathen. (Malachi 1:14).

Third Accusation Challenged

God rebuked the people for heathen marriages and divorce. As children of one Father, the chosen people were all brethren, but they wronged one another and profaned the sanctity to which their race is pledged by commonly taking in marriage the worshippers of heathen gods. Well-deserved punishment would fall on all who thus transgressed, for on this evil, another followed. The very altar of God was covered with the tears of the weeping women who flocked around it, and the offering was thereby rendered unacceptable. (2:11–13). Then came the challenge:

> And this have ye done again, covering the altar of the LORD with tears, with weeping, and with crying out, insomuch that he regards not the offering any more, or receiveth it with good will at your hand. Yet ye say, *Wherefore?* Because the LORD hath been witness between thee and the wife of thy youth, against whom thou hast dealt treacherously: yet is she thy compan-

ion, and the wife of thy covenant. And did not he make one? Yet had he the residue of the spirit. And wherefore one? That he might seek a godly seed. Therefore, take heed to your spirit, and let none deal treacherously against the wife of his youth. For the LORD, the God of Israel, saith that he hates putting away: for one covers violence with his garment, saith the LORD of hosts: therefore, take heed to your spirit, that ye deal not treacherously (Malachi 2:13–16).

Then came "How or when did we do such thing you have accused us of doing?" Pagan spouses and mixed children were found even in the priestly ranks. This calls to memory Ezra's ordeal.

And they made an end with all the men that had taken strange wives by the first day of the first month. And among the sons of the priests there were found that had taken strange wives: namely, of the sons of Jeshua the son of Jozadak, and his brethren; Maaseiah, and Eliezer, and Jarib, and Gedaliah. (Ezra 10:17–18).

Malachi's message came more than one hundred and fifty years after Ezra's time. Priests were still breaking the covenant that God had made with the house of Levi.

Fourth Accusation Challenged

The people had lost their moral compass. They were calling evil good and good things evil. Sounds very much like many today! Malachi told them that they had wearied God.

> Ye have wearied the LORD with your words. Yet ye say, *Wherein have we wearied him?* When ye say, Everyone that doeth evil is good in the sight of the LORD, and he delights in them; or Where is the God of judgment? (Malachi 2:17)

Paul warned Titus that some men would do this very thing in his day:

> Unto the pure all things are pure: but unto them that are defiled and unbelieving is nothing pure; but even their mind and conscience is defiled. They profess that they know God; but in works they deny him, being abominable, and disobedient, and unto every good work reprobate (Titus 1:15–16).

Malachi said they even mocked God by asking where was He? Peter echoed the same in his day:

> And saying, Where is the promise of his coming? for since the fathers fell asleep, all things continue as they were from the beginning of the creation (2 Peter 3:4).

One can easily see that these kinds of actions do weary God.

Fifth Accusation Challenged

"For I am the LORD, I change not; therefore, ye sons of Jacob are not consumed." Here Malachi pointed to Israel's rebellion against God and His covenant with them. Malachi reminded them that God never changes. When He establishes a covenant, He never breaks it. Israel should have known that from the times of David. David wrote in the Psalms,

> Also, I will make him my firstborn, higher than the kings of the earth. My mercy will I keep for him forevermore, and my covenant shall stand fast with him. His seed also will I make to endure forever, and his throne as the days of heaven. If his children forsake my law and walk not in my judgments. If they break my statutes and keep not my commandments. Then will I visit their transgression with the rod, and their iniquity with stripes; Nevertheless, my lovingkindness will I not utterly take from him, nor suffer my faithfulness to fail. My covenant will I not break, nor alter the thing that is gone out of my lips. Once have I sworn by my holiness that I will not lie unto David. His seed shall endure forever, and his throne as the sun before me. It shall be established forever as the moon, and as a faithful witness in heaven. Selah. But thou hast cast off and abhorred, thou hast been wroth with thine anointed. Thou hast made void the covenant of thy servant: thou hast profaned his crown by casting it to the ground (Psalm 89:27–39).

Jeremiah made a similar statement:

> Turn, O backsliding children, saith the LORD; for I
> am married unto you: and I will take you one of a city,
> and two of a family, and I will bring you to Zion (Jere-
> miah 3:14).

Malachi continued his complaint into the next verse:

> Even from the days of your fathers ye are gone away
> from mine ordinances and have not kept them. Return
> unto me, and I will return unto you, saith the LORD
> of hosts. But ye said, *Wherein shall we return?*
> (Malachi 3:7).

It seems that evil had consumed Israel so much that
they were blinded to their own sins; thus "Wherein shall
we return?" They seemed not to know that they were in a
lost condition. The prophet went immediately into the
next accusation to show why there was a need to return
to God.

Sixth Accusation Challenged

> Will a man rob God? Yet ye have robbed me. But ye
> say, *Wherein have we robbed thee?* In tithes and offer-
> ings (Malachi 1:8).

Here the prophet unleashed the strong and shaming
charge against Israel. From the long-continued course of
rebellion, in which, but for the fact that "Jehovah changes

not" they would long since have been "consumed," they were called upon to return to the path of obedience (v. 7). The charge against them, which they insolently and repeatedly challenged, was brought home to them in the definite shape of "robbing God," and that in "tithes' and offerings" (v. 8). The "curse" was their wages as a nation (v. 9); but the way of blessing was open to them still (v. 10). The curse could yet be rolled away (v. 11) so that blessing eminent and conspicuously would succeed in its place (v. 12). They must return to God and cease robbing Him.

Seventh Accusation Challenged

> Your words have been stout against me, saith the LORD. Yet ye say, *What have we spoken so much against thee?* (Malachi 3:13).

The prophet now poured out the warning of God's judgment. The righteous judgment of God is displayed here in this passage. Malachi repeated the charge of open impiety, which he had already made (2:17), and mets their virtual denial of it in verse 13 by repeating the disrespectful language that they used (v. 14) in the profane conclusion that they drew (v. 15). Malachi pointed out the converse among them of the godly remnant and declared that even now the righteous Judge discerned between the two. Already, "names are written in heaven" of those whom He will claim for His own in the day of His discriminating action (vv. 16–17). In other passages, we find God's book mentioned. In the book of Exodus, we find:

> Yet now, if thou wilt forgive their sin; and if not, blot me, I pray thee, out of thy book which thou hast written. (Exodus 32:32).

Also, Paul wrote of this book of God's records:

> And I entreat thee also, true yokefellow, help those women which labored with me in the gospel, with Clement also, and with other my fellow laborers, whose names are in the book of life. (Philippians 4:3).

On that day all men shall "return" from their wanderings in doubt and defiance and acknowledge the justice of the discerning sentence. (v. 18). For while the wicked shall be consumed as with the breath of a furnace (4:1–3), on the righteous the sun of righteousness shall arise with beneficent and healing power, restoring them to joyful liberty (v. 2) and making them triumphant over their foes (v. 3). Just as the same sun hardens the clay and melts the wax, God's righteousness deals harshly with sinners and mercifully with the righteous.

Conclusion of the Book

With the certainty of a future so desirable, they are called upon, by loving obedience to the Law which God has given them (4:4), and in expectation of the final precursor—"Elijah's coming," before "the great and terrible day," to whom He promises to avert the threatened curse (5, 6). See the following:

> Behold, I will send you Elijah the prophet before the coming of the great and dreadful day of the LORD: And he shall turn the heart of the fathers to the children, and the heart of the children to their fathers, lest I come and smite the earth with a curse (Malachi 4:5–6).

Matthew addresses this coming of Elijah:

> And Jesus answered and said unto them, Elijah truly shall first come, and restore all things. But I say unto you, That Elijah is come already, and they knew him not, but have done unto him whatsoever they listed. Likewise, shall also the Son of man suffer of them. Then the disciples understood that he spake unto them of John the Baptist (Matthew 17:11–13).

The phrase "with a curse" has been debated. Just where was it supposed to be in this chapter? The Masoretic direction is to read it a second time at the book's ending (Malachi 4:5) in order to avoid concluding with the ominous word "curse" or "ban," and the LXX, presumably with the same object, rearranges the verse and places Malachi 4:4 after Malachi 4:5–6. Yet the dark close of the Old Testament, "Lest I come and smite with the curse," rightly understood, is the truest preparation for the bright opening of the New Testament, "Behold, I am come to bless!"

Discussion Questions

1. What was the object of the book?
2. What was the only complaint about God's positive action?
3. How were the priests robbing God?
4. Who was the second Elijah, and what was His purpose?

Scripture Index

Credits

Contributors

Bill Bagents (DMin Amridge University) is Professor of Ministry, Counseling and Biblical Studies at Heritage Christian University, Florence, Alabama, USA.

Kaleb Baker (pursing MMin) is Admissions Counselor at Heritage Christian University, Florence, Alabama, USA.

Jeremy Barrier (PhD Brite Divinity School, Texas Christian University) is Professor of Biblical Literature at Heritage Christian University, Florence, Alabama, USA.

Ismael Berlanga (DMin Lincoln Christian University) serves as an Army Chaplain and Certified Chaplain Clinician at the United States Disciplinary Barracks at Fort Leavenworth, KS. He and Brigette have been married for 16 years and are members of the Roswell Church of Christ in Kansas City, KS. He is the author of *Imperative: Studies from the Book of James* (*Cypress Publications,* 2022).

Ed Gallagher (PhD Hebrew Union College) is Professor of Christian Scripture at Heritage Christian University, Florence, Alabama, USA.

Justin Guin (MDiv Freed-Hardeman University) is Adjunct Instructor at Heritage Christian University, Florence, Alabama, USA. He has served the Double Springs Church of Christ (Double Springs, Alabama) as the youth/associate minister since 2004.

Todd Johnston (MMin Heritage Christian University) serves as Executive Director for the Tennessee Children's Home—West Campus in Pinson, Tennessee, USA.

Wayne Kilpatrick (MAR Harding School of Theology) is emeritus professor of church history at Heritage Christian University, Florence, Alabama, USA.

Tim Martin (PhD Amridge University) is the Education Minister for the Mt. Juliet Church of Christ, Mt. Juliet, Tennessee, USA.

Zack Martin (pursuing PhD at Midwestern Baptist Theological Seminary) is Instructor of Historical Theology at Heritage Christian University, Florence, Alabama, USA.

Clay McFerrin (MBA, Tennessee Technological University) is Director of Institutional Effectiveness at HCU.

Andrew Phillips (PhD Regent University) is an Adjunct Instructor at Heritage Christian University, Florence, Alabama, USA. He has preached for the Graymere Church of Christ in Columbia, TN since 2011.

Baron Vander Maas (MA Harding School of Theology) is the Minister at Mt. Zion Church of Christ, Florence, Alabama, USA.

Berean Study Series

Future Berean Study Series Titles

Upcoming themes for the Berean Study Series are:

The Bond of Peace: The Seven Ones from Ephesians 4 (2026)

Someone Is Coming: Prophecies of Jesus (2027)

Someone Is Here: Teachings of Jesus (2028)

Someone Is Coming Again: Return of Jesus (2029)

Cypress Publications

Onesimus
Bible Study Series

To see full catalog of Heritage Christian University Press
and its imprint Cypress Publications, visit
www.hcu.edu/publications